CELEBRITY SIGHTING

MELVIN J. BAGLEY

CELEBRITY SIGHTING

A Collection of Letters from Famous People

TATE PUBLISHING
AND ENTERPRISES, LLC

Published by Tate Publishing & Enterprises, LLC
127 E. Trade Center Terrace | Mustang, Oklahoma 73064 USA
1.888.361.9473 | www.tatepublishing.com

Tate Publishing is committed to excellence in the publishing industry. The company reflects the philosophy established by the founders, based on Psalm 68:11,
"The Lord gave the word and great was the company of those who published it."

Book design copyright © 2014 by Tate Publishing, LLC. All rights reserved.
Cover design by Joel Uber
Interior design by Jomar Ouano

Published in the United States of America

ISBN: 978-1-62994-513-2
Biography & Autobiography / General
14.03.20

DEDICATION

I dedicate the book to May Sandico Holland because without her, this book would not be possible.

I would like to dedicate this book to all the famous people who donated their eyeglasses to my museum.

CONTENTS

PREFACE

As a practicing optometrist in the early 1960s, I knew that a majority of the population wore glasses. Thinking of all the movie stars, politicians, and other famous people that wore glasses, I came up with the idea to try and collect famous people's eyeglasses to be displayed in the waiting room of my office.

I enlisted the help of my four daughters to type letters to all sorts of prominent people all over the world. Over a span of almost thirty years I received over one hundred fifty pairs of glasses which I thereafter displayed in "The Famous People's Eye Glasses Museum". In addition, I received several hundred letters from the people who sent their glasses and I also received letters explaining that the person did not wear glasses or why they could not send their glasses, which I found very interesting. In this book I share some of those letters and my own personal comments about some of the letters.

What I started and thought might be a crazy idea turned into a one-of-a-kind museum. I found the information shared by those sending glasses or writing me back very interesting and I hope in reading this book you will find it equally interesting.

—Dr. Melvin J Bagley

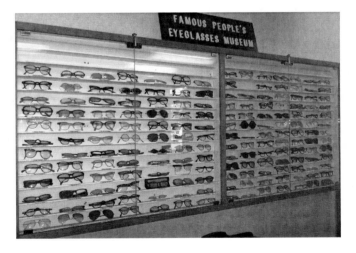

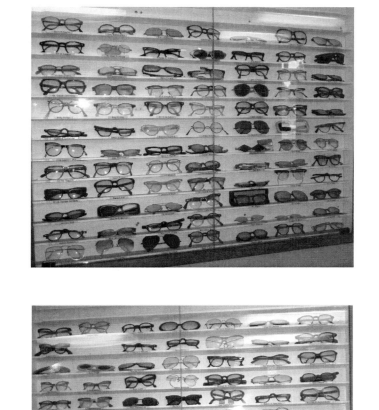

RONALD REAGAN
Fortieth President of the United States

40th President of the United States, in office January 20,
  1981 – January 20, 1989
33rd Governor of California, in office January 2, 1967–
  January 6, 1975

Birth Name:	Ronald Wilson Reagan
Born:	February 6, 1911
	Tampico Illinois, US
Died:	June 5, 2004 (aged 93)
	Los Angeles, California, US
Political Party:	Republican (1963-2004)
Other Political:	Democratic (before 1962)
Education:	Bachelor of Arts degree in Economics and Sociology.
Nationality:	American
Marriage:	Jane Wyman in 1938 to 1949, Nancy Davis 1952 to his death
Children with Jane:	Maureen and Christine, Adopted Michael
Children with Nancy:	Patti and Ron

When I wrote and asked Ronald Reagan for
his pair of glasses. He was still the Governor of
California. I was elated when he wrote me such
a wonderful letter. As I followed his career as

President, all the things he did made the letter that he sent to me more important. I can honestly say this letter, of all letters, accompanying glasses in my museum makes me proud.

The best thing that Reagan did was to introduce Reaganomics. Reagonomics includes lowering the unemployment, and stimulating the economy with large across-the-board tax cuts. Sixteen million new jobs were created and prices of oil dropped to ensure America's economic strength.[1]

FAITH BALDWIN

Born:	October 1, 1893
	New Rochelle, New York
Died:	March 18, 1978 (age 84)
	Norwalk, Connecticut
Occupation:	Novelist
Nationality:	American
Period:	1920s–1970s
Genres:	Romance, Women's Fiction

I first found out about Faith Baldwin by watching "Faith Baldwin Romance Theater". I was immediately impressed by her talent. I was certainly happy when we received a letter from her.

Faith Baldwin was a very successful United States author of romance, fiction and novels on women juggling career and family life. She published over 100 novels in her lifetime that completes a five foot shelf. She continued to write until her death. Her life philosophy "It is in God and His spirit in mankind. It is in man and was his struggle. It is in the Golden Rule and in the valor of men, however ignoble their shortcomings."[2]

Melvin J. Bagley

FAITH BALDWIN
ROUTE 2, WEED AVENUE
NORWALK, CONNECTICUT

Dear Dr Bagley;I am mailing you
first class regular mail a pair of glasses.I must
say your hobby astounds me;why not hearing aids
or dentures(I dont wear either)

I wear distance glasses and
reading glasses,I cant wear bi focals.Hence I have
2 pair distance and 2 for reading and one pair of
distance sunglasses.My RX was changed a year or so
ago but as the change was very slight I saved one of
the old pairs(distance) which is what I am sending you
--no one in their right mind could afford to send
any he or she is currently wearing what witÿh the cost
⟨ frames as well as lenses.

I enclose a card for authenticity,whatever
that is..anyway as I love Nevada I could not refuse
you

24

IRVING BERLIN

Birth name:	Israel Isidore Baline (Beilin)
Born:	May 11, 1888
	Near Mogilev, Russian Empire (modern day Belarus)
Died:	September 22, 1989 (age 101)
	New York City, New York, United States
Cause of Death:	Natural Death in his sleep.
Genres:	Broadway musicals, revues, show tunes
Occupations:	Songwriter, Composer, Lyricist
Years active:	1907-1971
Marriage:	Dorothy Goetz. She died six months later of typhoid fever.
	Ellin Mackay,
Children:	Mary Ellin Barrett; Elizabeth Irving Peters; and Linda Louise Emmet.

What I remember must about Irving Berlin is his struggle to make sure the song writers were adequately compensated for their contribution to the music world.

His family immigrated to Belarus when he was five years old. By the time he was thirteen his father passed away. The family helped out. To make a living, he was a newspaper boy and due to being in the streets, he got interested in music. He became a singing waiter and in his spare time he taught himself to play the piano. In the sixty year career he wrote about 1,500 songs for 19 broadway shows and 18 Hollywood films, some of his most famous songs are "Easter Parade," "White Christmas," "Happy Holidays," "This Is the Army Mr. Jones," "God Bless America," and "Always."

He is considered one of the greatest songwriters in American History.[3]

IRVING BERLIN *Music Corporation*
1650 BROADWAY, NEW YORK 19, N. Y. ● TELEPHONE CIRCLE 7·4200

May 28th, 1962

Dr. M. J. Bagley
Famous People's Eye Glasses Museum
61 East Frontier Blvd.
Henderson, Nevada

Dear Dr. Bagley:

Your letter of May 23rd has been received.

Mr. Berlin does not have a spare pair of eye glasses at this time. Should a pair become available, I'm sure Mr. Berlin will be glad to send them on to you.

Sincerely,

HILDA SCHNEIDER
Sec'y to Mr. Berlin

ELEANOR ROOSEVELT

Birth name:	Anna Eleanor Roosevelt
Born:	October 11, 1884
Died:	November 7, 1962
Cause of Death:	Aplastic Anemia and Cardiac Failure
Occupation:	Chairman of the Presidential Commission on the Status of Women
	January 20, 1966-November 7, 1962
	United States Delegate to the United Nation General Assembly
	December 31, 1946-1951
	United States Representative to the United Nations Commission on Human Rights, 1947-1953
	First Lady of the United States, March 4, 1933-April 12, 1945
Marriage:	Franklin D. Roosevelt
Children:	Anna Eleanor, James, Franklin Delano Jr. who died after 8 months, Elliott, Franklin Delano, Jr. and John Aspinwall II.

When I received this letter written personally from Eleanor, I was very happy. Imagine receiving a letter form one of the Greatest First Ladies who has ever lived personally writing a letter to me.

Eleanor is the longest serving First Lady of the United States, holding a post from 1933 to 1945 during her husband's fourth term in office.

Eleanor was a controversial first Lady for her outspokenness, particularly for her stands on racial issues. She was the first Lady to hold press conferences, write a syndicated newspaper column and speak at a National Convention. She was an advocate for expanding roles for women in the workplace, the civil rights of African American and Asian American women, and the rights of World War II refugees.

After the death of her husband she remained active in politics for the rest of her life. By the time she died, she was regarded as one of the most esteemed women in the world and the object of almost universal respect.[4]

MRS. FRANKLIN D. ROOSEVELT
55 EAST 74TH STREET
NEW YORK CITY 21, N. Y.

May 26, 1962

Dear Dr. Bagley:

I wish I could send you a pair of eye glasses for your collection. Unfortunately, however, I do not have any except the ones I am now using for reading.

With many regrets,

Very sincerely yours,

Eleanor Roosevelt

PEARL S. BUCK

Born:	June 26, 1892
	Hillsboro, West Virginia, United States
Died:	March 6, 1973 (aged 80)
	Danby, Vermont, United States
Cause of Death:	Lung Cancer
Occupation:	Writer, Teacher
Nationality:	American
Notable award(s)	Pulitzer Prize 1932
	Nobel Prize in Literature 1938
Spouse(s)	John Lossing Buck (1917-1 935)
	Richard Walsh (1935-1960) until his death

Any time we received a pair of glasses from an important person like Pearl Sydenstricker Buck, it was party time in the office, where the famous eyeglasses museum is located.

Born of missionaries parents, she moved to China when she was a child until she was 42 years old. She learned English through her mother. She learned to write through the influence of her Chinese friends who are prominent writers Xu Zhimo and Lin Yutang. They encouraged her to think of herself as a professional writer.

Her daughter Carol needed long term medical help. This inspired her to write They encouraged her to write *The Good Earth,* which won prizes.

One of her greatest contributions to society was the establishment of Welcome House, Inc. and the Opportunity House. The purpose was to publicize and eliminate injustices and prejudices suffered by children who because of their birth, were not permitted to enjoy the educational, social economic and civil privileges normally accorded to children born of Asian women left behind by the American soldiers based in Asia.

Buck's life was a combination of multiple careers of wife, mother, editor and political activist.[5]

R.R. 1 - BOX 164
PERKASIE, PENNSYLVANIA

June 11, 1962

Dear Dr. Bagley:

I have your letter and will send you a pair of my old glasses.

Sincerely yours,

Pearl S. Buck

Dr. M. J. Bagley
Famous People's Eye Glasses Museum
61 East Frontier Blvd.
Henderson, Nevada

PSB HS

HENRY FORD II
Chief Executive Officer of the Ford Motor Company 1945-1979

Born:	September 4, 1917
	Detroit, Michigan, US
Died:	September 29, 1987 (aged 70)
	Detroit Michigan
Cause of Death:	Pneumonia
Spouse(s)	Anne McDonnell, 1940-1964 (divorced)
	Maria Cristina Veltore, 1965-1980 (divorced)
	Kathleen DuRoss 1980-1987 (his death)
Relations:	Edsel Fort (Father)
	Eleanor Clay Ford (Mother)
Children:	Charlotte, Anne, and Edsel ford II (with McDonnell) Stepchildren, Deborah Guibord and Kimberly DuRoss (with Kathleen DuRoss.
Occupation:	Former Chairman and President and CEO of the Ford Motor Company

Everybody that owned a car around 1930 probably owned a Ford. Ford was able to produce cars on a production line, the first of its kind. I was happy to have anyone with the Ford name send eyeglasses to my museum.

Henry Ford II, or "Hank the Deuce", or "HF2", was the oldest son of Edsel Ford and the oldest grandson of Henry Ford, founder of Ford Motor Inc.

In 1943, his father, then the President of Ford Motors, died of cancer. He was serving in the navy thus unable to assume the responsibilities at the time. His grandfather Henry Ford took over the operation. At that time he no longer had the ability to run the company which cost the company millions of dollars. Two years later, he came home from the service, and the first thing he did was to fire Harry Bennett, head of the Ford Service Department. Acknowledging his inexperience, he hired several seasoned executives to support him, which included Ernest Breech and Lewis Crusoe and the ten young up and comers known as the Whiz Kids. Two of the them, Arjay Miller and Robert Mcnamara, went on to serve as presidents of Ford. A third member, J Edward Lundy, served in key financial roles for several decades and helped to establish Ford Finance's reputation as one of the best in the world.

He was awarded the Presidential Medal of Freedom from President Lyndon Johnson in 1969. Ford was inducted into the Junior Achievement U.S. Business Hall of Fame in 1996.[6]

Ford Motor Company

OFFICE OF THE CHAIRMAN

THE AMERICAN ROAD
DEARBORN, MICHIGAN
July 6,
1962

Dr. M. J. Bagley,
Director,
Famous People's Eye Glasses Museum,
61 East Frontier Blvd.,
Henderson, Nevada.

Dear Dr. Bagley:

Since Mr. Ford is in Europe
for a series of business meetings, I am
taking the liberty to acknowledge your
letter of June 20 concerning the desire
of the Museum to add to its collection
eye glasses worn by Mr. Ford and his
father, Mr. Edsel B. Ford.

I am sorry that it is not
possible to accommodate this request.
Mr. Ford's father did not wear glasses,
and Mr. Ford does not.

Yours very truly,

James Cummins
Office of Henry Ford II

NAT KING COLE

Birth name:	Nathaniel Adams Coles
Born:	March 17, 1919
	Montgomery, Alabama, US
Died:	February 15, 1965 (age 45)
	Santa Monica, California, US
Cause of Death:	Cancer
Genres:	Vocal jazz, swing, traditional pop, bolero.
Occupations:	Vocalist, pianist
Instruments:	Piano, vocals, guitar
Years Active:	1935-1965
Labels:	Decca, Capitol
Associated Acts:	Natalie Cole, Frank Sinatra, Dean Martin
Marriage:	Nadine Robinson divorced
	Maria Hawkins Ellington
Children:	Natalie, Carole, Nat Kelly Cole, Casey and Timolin.
Legacy:	Alabama Music Hall of Fame
	Alabama Jazz Hall of Fame
	Grammy Lifetime Achievement Award 1990
	Down beat Jazz Hall of Fame 1997
	Hit Parade Hall of fame 1994
	Rock and Roll Hall of Fame 2000

What a voice—soft, mellow, and very distinctive. Even though he did not send glasses, I was happy to hear that he did not wear glasses.

Nat King Cole started his career in a trio with Oscar Moore on the guitar and Wesley Prince on the double bass. They played until the late 1930s, where he was the pianist and the leader of the band.

In 1946 his career started when the Cole trio paid their own 15 minutes radio program on the air called King Cole Trio Time, which was the first radio program sponsored by a black performing artist. His most popular songs were "Nature Boy," "Mona Lisa," "Too Young," "Unforgettable," "After Midnight," and "When I fall In Love."

In 1956 he started the Nat King Cole Show. This was the first variety program hosted by an African American which created controversy at the time. Due to the lack of sponsorship, it only lasted a year.

Cole fought racism all his life and rarely performed in segregated venues. He also supported Senator John F. Kennedy and Lyndon Johnson.

Cole was a heavy smoker throughout his life he believed that smoking up to three packs a day gave his voice its rich sound.[7]

Melvin J. Bagley

449 SOUTH BEVERLY DRIVE • BEVERLY HILLS • CALIFORNIA

June 11,1962

Dr.M.J.Bagley
Famous People's Eye Glasses Museum
61 East Frontier Blvd.
Henderson,Nevada

Dear Dr.Bagley:

In answer to your letter in
which you requested a pair of Mr.
Cole's glasses, please be informed
that - fortunately - Mr. Cole does
not wear glasses.

With best wishes, I am

Very truly yours,

(Mrs.) Charlotte Sullivan
Secretary

36

BING CROSBY

Birth name:	Harry Lillis Cosby Jr.
Born:	May 3, 1903
	Tacoma WA U S
Died:	October 14, 1977 age: 74
	La Moraleja, Alcobenda
	Madrid, Spain
Genres:	Traditional pop, jazz, vocal
Occupations:	Singer, actor
Instruments:	Vocals
Years active:	1926-1977
Labels:	Brunswick, Decca, Reprise, RCA Victor, Verve, United Artists
Associated:	Brunswick, Decca, Reprise, RCA Victor, Verve, United Artists Bob Hope, Dixie Lee, Peggy Lee, Dean Martin, Frank Sinatra, Fred Astaire, the Rhythm Boys, Rosemary, Clooney, David Bowie, Louis Armstrong

I personally met Bing Crosby in his later years on one of his hunting expeditions, and I was able to thank him personally for sending his eyeglasses to the museum.

Bing Crosby was an American singer and actor. His trademark bass-baritone voice made him one of the best-selling recording artist, over half a billion records in circulation.

Bing Crosby's contribution to the music industry was the development of equipment and recording techniques such as the Laugh Track which is still in use today. He left NBC to work with ABC because NBC was not interested in recording at the time, but ABC accepted him and his new ideas. He was the first performer to pre-record his radio shows and master his commercial recordings onto magnetic tape.

He is one of the 22 people to have three stars on the Hollywood Walk of Fame as follows: Motion Picture, Radio and Audio Recording.[8]

Bing Crosby

Hollywood

July 9, 1962

Dr. M. J. Bagley, Director
FAMOUS PEOPLE'S EYE GLASSES MUSEUM
61 East Frontier Boulevard
Henderson, Nevada

Dear Dr. Bagley:

Am forwarding under separate cover a pair of my eye glasses for your FAMOUS PEOPLE'S EYE GLASSES MUSEUM, as you requested.

All best good wishes -

Sincerely,

Bing Crosby

Bing Crosby

GREER GARSON

Birth name:	Eileen Evelyn Greer Garson
Born:	29 September 1904
	Manor Park, Essex, England
	United Kingdom
Died:	6 April 1996 (aged 91)
	Dallas, Texas, United States
Cause of Death:	Heart Failure
Nationality:	British
Occupation:	Actress
Years Active:	1937-1982
Spouse(s)	Edward Alec Abbot Snelson (1933-1943)
	Richard Ney (1943-1947)
	Buddy Fogelson (1949-1987 his death)
Religion:	Presbyterian

What a beautiful letter I received with her glasses. What she wrote in her letter about rose colored glasses is certainly a very philosophic view of how people should view the world.

Greer Garson was a British actress who was very popular during World War II. Garson received seven Academy Award nominations, winning the Best Actress award for the movie Mrs. Miniver. She later on married the leading man in the movie Mrs. Miniver, Richard Ney. Due to the age difference of her being 12 years his senior, the marriage only lasted four years. In 1949 she married a millionaire, Texas oilman and horse breeder, E. E. Buddy Fogelson.

She donated millions of dollars for the construction of the Greer Garson theatre at both the Santa Fe University of Art and Design and at Southern Methodist University's Meadow School of Art. Three conditions needed to be met: first she the stage to be circular, second the premiere production was to be William Shakepeare's *A Midsummer Night's Dream* and third they were to have large ladies' rooms.[9]

GREER GARSON

July 10, 1962

Dr. M. J. Bagley, Director
Famous People's Eye Glasses Museum
61 East Frontier Blvd.
Henderson, Nevada

Dear Dr. Bagley:

In reply to your request, here is a pair of old sun glasses, which is all I have to offer, but you are welcome to add them to your unique collection.

If I had an actual pair, I would like to have sent you some rose-colored spectacles, just to encourage folks to take the cheerful view!

There is such a surprising variety in eye wear styles and devices, from lorgnettes to goggles, that I am sure your exhibition must be quite fascinating. Especially with the personal touch you are contriving to add.

Every good wish.

Sincerely,

GREER GARSON

GG/kmp
Enc.

HEDDA HOPPER

Born:	Elda Furry
	May 2, 1885
	Holidaysburg, Pennsylvania
Died:	February 1, 1966 (aged 80)
	Hollywood, Los Angeles, California, US
Cause of Death:	Double Pneumonia
Resting Place:	Rose Hill Cemetery
Nationality:	American
Names:	Other Elder Furry
	Elder Milar
	Mrs. DeWolf Hopper
Occupation:	Actress, gossip columnist
Years active:	1908-1966
Known for:	Writing "Hedda Hopper's Hollywood"
Spouse(s):	DeWolf Hopper (m. 1913-1922)
Children:	William Hopper (1915-1970)

Back in the early days of gossip, when she was active in that business, I was always surprised where she could get her material for her gossip column, Hedda Hopper's Hollywood. I don't think anybody would ever top her sometimes scandalous goings-on in Hollywood.

She eventually ran away to New York City and began her career in the chorus on the Broadway stage and later joined the Hopper Company.

She had been an actress of stage and screen for years before being offered the chance to write the column "Hedda Hopper's Hollywood" for the *Los Angeles Times* in 1938.

She was known for hobnobbing with the biggest names in the industry, for getting a scoop before almost anyone else most of the time, and for being vicious in dealing with those who displeased her, whether intentionally or not.[10]

FAMOUS PEOPLE'S EYE GLASSES MUSEUM
61 EAST FRONTIER BLVD.
HENDERSON, NEVADA

July 24, 1962

Miss Hedda Hopper
6331 Hollywood Blvd.
Hollywood, Calif.

Dear Miss Hopper,

The FAMOUS PEOPLE'S EYE GLASSES MUSEUM would like to add a pair of your eye glasses to it's growing collection. It would be greatly appreciated by us if you would send us a pair of your old glasses, regardless of their condition, along with a letter attesting to their authenticity.

Thank You,

Dr. M. J. Bagley
Director

MJB/cmh

My dear Dr. Bagley:

I have not kept any eye glasses other than those I wear. Sorry. Thank you for thinking of me.

Yours,

Hedda Hopper

JENNIFER JONES

Actress

Born:	Phylis Lee lsley
	March 2, 1919
	Tulsa, Oklahoma
Died:	December 17, 2009 (aged 90)
	Malibu, California
Cause Of Death:	Natural Cause
Alma mater:	Northwestern University
Occupation:	Actress
Years active:	1939-1974
Spouse(s)	Robert Walker, David O. Selznick, Norton Simon
Children:	Robert Walker, Jr., Michael Walker, Mary Jennifer Selznick
	Awards Hollywood Walk of Fame at 6429 Hollywood Blvd.
	Academy Award for Best Actress
	Golden Globe Award for Best Actress-Motion Picture Drama

Anytime I received a letter from famous people who did not wear glasses, I was happy to receive a letter anyway. Even though I did not receive a letter from David O' Selznick, I included him since it was his secretary who wrote the letter.

Jennifer Jones started her career as part time modeling hats for the Powers Agency while looking for possible acting jobs. She auditioned for an acting role for David O' Selznick and was accepted and signed a seven year contract. While working with O'Selznick, the two had an affair that caused her separation from Robert Walker. She eventually married David O'Selznick until his death.[11]

DAVID O. SELZNICK
CULVER CITY, CALIFORNIA

July 27, 1962

Dr. M. J. Bagley, Director
Famous People's Eye Glasses Museum
61 East Frontier Blvd.
Henderson, Nevada

Dear Dr. Bagley:

I am replying on behalf of Miss Jones to your letter of July 24, 1962. We are sorry not to be able to concur with your request, since Miss Jones does not wear glasses.

Sincerely yours,

Lea Purwin
Secretary to David O. Selznick

DAVID O. SELZNICK

David O. Selznick, born on May 10, 1902 and died on June 22, 1965, was an American film producer. He is best known for having produced *Gone with the Wind* in 1939, *Rebecca* in 1940 and *The Third Man* in 1949, both the former earning him an Oscar for Best Picture.

In 1930, Selznick married Irene Gladys Mayer, daughter of MGM mogul Louis B. Mayer. They had two sons, Daniel and Jeffrey. They separated in 1945 and divorced in 1948. He died of heart attack at the age of 63.[12]

DAVID O. SELZNICK
CULVER CITY, CALIFORNIA

July 27, 1962

Dr. M. J. Bagley, Director
Famous People's Eye Glasses Museum
61 East Frontier Blvd.
Henderson, Nevada

Dear Dr. Bagley:

        I am replying on behalf of Miss Jones to your letter
of July 24, 1962. We are sorry not to be able to concur
with your request, since Miss Jones does not wear glasses.

                Sincerely yours,

                Lea Purwin
                Secretary to David O. Selznick

HELEN HAYES

Birth name	Helen Hayes Brown
Born:	October 10, 1900
	Washington, DC
Died:	March 17, 1992 (age 92)
	Nyack, New York
Cause of Death:	Congestive Heart Failure
Occupation:	Actress
Years active:	1904-1985
Spouse(s)	John Swanson (m 1926-1926 divorced)
	Charles MacArthur (m1928-1956; his death)

I was never very interested in Helen Hayes, but after receiving a pair of glasses from her for my museum, I began to follow her and learned about her, so now I am truly Helen Hayes fan.

Helen Hayes was an American actress for 70 years, the First Lady of the American Theater and was one of eleven people who have won a Emmy, Grammy, Oscar and Tony Award. She also received from President Reagan the Presidential Medal of Freedom, America's highest civilian honor in 1986. Since 1984, they have recognized excellence in professional theater in greater Washington, D.C., calling it the Helen Hayes Award.

Hayes wrote three memoirs: *A Gift of Joy*, *On Reflection* and *My Life in Three Acts*. Some of the themes in these books include her return to Roman Catholicism.

She has a star on the Hollywood walk of fame at 6220 Hollywood Blvd.[13]

HELEN HAYES

July 31, 1962

Dr. M. J. Bagley
Famous People's Eye Glasses Museum
61 East Frontier Blvd.
Henderson, Nevada

Dear Dr. Bagley,

Enclosed is a pair of
my old eyeglasses for your Museum.

All good wishes,

Helen Hayes

J. EDGAR HOOVER

Birth name	John Edgar Hoover
Born	January 1, 1895
	Washington, DC US
Died:	May 2, 1972 (aged 77)
	Washington, DC US
Cause of Death:	Heart Attack attributed to Cardiovascular disease
Religion:	Presbyterian
Education:	Law Degree from George Washington University Law school 1916
	1ST Director of the Federal Bureau of Investigation
In Office:	1935
President:	Franklin D. Roosevelt
	Harry S. Truman
	Dwight D. Eisenhower
	John F. Kennedy
	Lyndon B. Johnson
	Richard Nixon

In my youth I did not know too much about the FBI, but I did know that Edgar Hoover was the one person instrumental in making the great success it has become.

Hoover was the first Director of the Federal Bureau of Investigation FBI. He was credited with building the FBI into a larger crime-fighting agency and with instituting a number of modernizations to police technology, such as a centralized fingerprinting file and forensic laboratories.[14]

OFFICE OF THE DIRECTOR

UNITED STATES DEPARTMENT OF JUSTICE

FEDERAL BUREAU OF INVESTIGATION

WASHINGTON 25, D.C.

August 1, 1962

Dr. M. J. Bagley
Director
Famous People's Eye
   Glasses Museum
61 East Frontier Boulevard
Henderson, Nevada

Dear Dr. Bagley:

      Your letter of July 24th was received as Mr. Hoover was preparing to depart the city. He asked me to advise you that he has not retained any of his old eyeglasses and therefore is unable to comply with your request.

Sincerely yours,

Helen Gandy

Helen W. Gandy
Secretary

DREW PEARSON
Journalist

Birth name	Andrew Russell "Drew" Pearson
Born:	December 13, 1897
	Evanston, Illinois
Died:	September 1, 1969.
Cause of Death:	Heart Attack

Drew Pearson always appealed to me I think because of his unusual name.

Drew Pearson was one of the best known American columnist of his day, noted for his syndicated newspaper column "Washington Merry-Go-Round." He also had a program on NBC Radio called Drew Pearson Comments. The column was syndicated to more than twice as many as any other, with an estimated 60 million readers, and was famous for its investigative style of journalism.[15]

D R E W   P E A R S O N
WASHINGTON   MERRY - GO - ROUND
1313 Twenty-ninth St., N.W. Washington 7, D. C.

August 2, 1962

Dr. M. J. Bagley
Director
Famous People's Eye
    Glasses Museum
61 East Frontier Blvd.
Henderson, Nevada

Dear Dr. Bagley:

Thank you so much for your letter of July 30th. Mr. Pearson
is in Europe at the present time
and is not expected back until
the end of this month. However,
he is one of those fortunate people who has only one pair of glasses -- his first -- and therefore
has none to spare for your museum.
We certainly will keep you in mind,
though, and I know he will appreciate your interest in adding his
eye glasses to your famous collection.

Sincerely,

Dagmar M. Miller

Dagmar M. Miller
Secretary

DUNCAN HINES

Born:	March 26, 1880
	Bowling Green, Kentucky, US
Died:	March 15, 1959 (aged 78)
	Bowling Green, Kentucky, US
Occupation:	Businessman, writer, food critic

Apparently we were a little late on our letter, since it was received after he passed away. I was delighted to receive a letter form Mrs. Clara Hines on his behalf for our museum.

Duncan Hines was a traveling salesman for a Chicago printer. In 1935 at the age of 55, he had eaten a lot of good and bad meals on the road across the United States. In the same year, and due to his traveling and eating all over, he was able to put a book together called *Adventures of Good Eating*, which highlighted restaurants and their featured dishes that Hines had personally enjoyed in locations across America.[16]

Mrs. Duncan Hines
728 Richland Drive
Bowling Green, Kentucky   August 3, 1962

Dr. M. J. Bagley, Director
Famous People's Eye Glasses Museum
61 East Frontier Boulevard
Henderson, Nevada

Dear Dr. Bagley:

I have your letter of July 24th addressed to my late
husband requesting a pair of his glasses for your museum.

I regret that I am unable to comply with your request, for
I have long since disposed of his glasses and do not have
anything I could send you.

Sincerely

Clara H. Hines

Mrs. Duncan Hines

GENE KELLY

Birth name	Eugene Curran Kelly
Born:	August 23, 1912
	Pittsburgh, Pennsylvania, U.S.
Died:	February 2, 1996 (aged 83)
	Beverly Hills, California, U.S.
Cause of Death:	Complications from stroke
Resting Place:	Cremated
Nationality:	American
Education:	Peabody High School
Alma mater:	Pennsylvania State College
	University of Pittsburgh
	University of Pittsburgh School of Law
Occupation:	Actor, dancer, singer, director, producer, choreographer
Years active:	1938-1994
Marriage:	Betsy Blair
	Jeanne Coyne
	Patricia Ward
Children:	Kerry from Betsy Blair
	Bridget and Tim from Jeanne Coyne

Whenever I receive a letter like this from a very famous person, it always surprises me how many people in this position do not have spare glasses.

Gene Kelly was known for his energetic dancing style, good looks and likeable characters he played on screen. He was an Irish-American dancer, actor, singer, film director, producer and choreographer.

Kelly's first career breakthrough was in *The Time of Your Life*, which opened in 1939, where the first time on Broadway he danced to his own choreography.

Kelly was the recipient of an Academy Honorary Award in 1952 for his career achievements. He later received lifetime achievement awards in the Kennedy Center Honors, and from the Screen Actors Guild and American Film Institute in 1999. The American Film Institute also numbered him 15th in their Greatest Male Stars of All Time list.

Kelly's health declined steadily in the late 1980s. A stroke in 1994 and another stroke in 1995 left him mostly bedridden. In 1996, he died in his sleep.[17]

725 NORTH RODEO DRIVE
BEVERLY HILLS, CALIFORNIA

August 3, 1962

Dr. M. J. Bagley
61 East Frontier Blvd.
Henderson, Nevada

Dear Dr. Bagley:

Thank you for your letter of July 24th requesting a pair of my old eye glasses.

The only trouble is that I have only recently started wearing glasses and I just don't have any old ones. I have just the two pair and need them both for different purposes.

Regretfully,

Gene Kelly

OZZIE NELSON

Birth name	Oswald George Nelson
Born	March 20, 1906
	Jersey City, New Jersey US
Died:	June 3, 1975 (aged 69)
	Hollywood, Los Angeles
	California US
Cause of Death:	Liver cancer
Resting Place:	Forest Lawn Memorial Park, Hollywood Hills
Education:	Ridgefield Park High School
Alma mater:	Rutgers University, Rutgers School of Law-Newark
Occupation:	Actor, band leader, television producer and director
Spouse(s):	Harriet Hilliard (1909-1994)
Children:	David Nelson (1936-2011)
	Ricky Nelson (1940-1985)
Relatives:	Tracy Nelson (granddaughter)
	Matthew Nelson (grandson)
	Gunnar Nelson (grandson)
	Sam Nelson (grandson)

I honestly did not know much about Ozzie Nelson when he was alive, however I have become a great fan of his grandchildren Matthew and Gunnar Nelson.

Ozzie Nelson started his entertainment career as a band leader. He formed and led the Ozzie Nelson Band.

In 1935, Ozzie married the band's vocalist Harriet Hilliard. The couple had two children, David, who became an actor and director and Eric "Ricky" became an actor and a singer.

In the 1940s Nelson began to look for ways to spend time with his family, especially his growing sons. He then developed and produced his own radio series, *The Adventure of Ozzie and Harriet,* and in 1952 it moved over to television. The show starred the entire family, and America watched Ozzie and Harriet raise their boys. Nelson was producer and co-writer of the entire series. He was very hands-on and involved with every aspect of the radio and then TV program.

Ozzie Nelson has a star on the Hollywood walk of Fame at 6555 Hollywood Boulevard for his contribution to the television industry and one with his wife Harriet at 6260 Hollywood Boulevard for their contribution to radio.[18]

August 8, 1962

Dear Dr. Bagley:

Thank you for your nice letter of
July 30. It was most thoughtful of
you to think of me in connection with
your "Famous People's Eye Glasses
Museum."

Enclosed are a pair of my glasses and
I am pleased to have them join your
collection.

Sincerely yours,

EDWARD R. MURROW

Birth name	Egbert Roscoe Murrow
Born	April 25, 1908
	Guilford, County
	North Carolina US
Died:	April 27, 1965 (aged 57)
	Pawling, New York
Cause of Death:	Lung Cancer
Alma mater:	Washington State–1930
Occupation:	Journalist, Radio broadcaster
Spouse(s)	Janet Huntington Brewster (1935-65)
Children:	Charles Casey Murrow
Parents:	Roscoe Conkin Murrow
	Ethel Murrow

My recollection of Ed Murrow was his mellow voice and his clever way of signing off his news broadcast to receive his letter two and a half years. Edward R. Murrow was an American broadcast journalist. He first came to prominence with a series of radio news broadcasts during World War II, which were followed by millions of listeners in the United States.

Born at Polecat Creek, North Carolina his parents were Quakers. The youngest of three brothers and was a mixture of different descents; English, Scots, Irish and German. He attended high school in nearby Edison, and he was the president of the student body in his senior year and excelled on the debate team in Skagit County in Western Washington.

In 1929, he attended the National student Federation of America convention. Murrow gave a speech urging college students to become more interested in national and word affairs, this led to his election as president of the federation. In 1930 he earned a Bachelor's degree in Speech and moved to New York.

Murrow joined CBS as a director of talks and eduction in 1935 and remained with the network for his entire career. In 1937 he went to London to serve as the director of CBS's European operations. Murrow gained his first glimpse of fame during the March 1938 Anschluss, in which Adolf Hitler engineered the annexation of Austria by Nazi Germany. Murrow put together a European News Roundup of reaction to the Anschluss, which brought correspondents from various European cities together for a single broadcast.

He first worked on the radio show called "Hear It Now" and later on television as "See It Now", "Person to Person" and "Small World."

Murrow resigned form CBS to accept a position as head of the United States Information Agency, parent of the Voice of America, in 1961 for President John F. Kennedy.[19]

UNITED STATES INFORMATION AGENCY
WASHINGTON

OFFICE OF
THE DIRECTOR

August 15, 1962

Dear Dr. Bagley:

     Right now I have no old pair of glasses. When
I get new glasses I will be glad to send you the ones I
now use if you are still interested.

               Sincerely,

               Edward R. Murrow
               Director

Dr. M. J. Bagley
Director
Famous People's Eye Glasses Museum
61 East Frontier Blvd.
Henderson, Nevada

CARY GRANT

Born:	Archibald Alexander Leach
	January 18, 1904
	Bristol, England United Kingdom
Died:	November 29, 1986 (aged 82)
	Davenport, Iowa, USA
Cause of Death:	Cerebral Hemorrhage
Education:	Bishop Road Primary School Fairfield Grammar School
Occupation:	Actor
Years Active:	1932-1966
Spouse(s):	Virginia Cherrill, Barbara Hutton, Betsy Drake, Dyan Cannon,Barbara Harris
Partners:	Maureen Donaldson
Children:	Lance Reventlow, Jennifer Grant
Awards:	Academy Honorary Award

Wow imagine getting a pair of glasses from a movie star of his magnitude. Cary Grant was an English film and stage actor, who later gained American citizenship known for his transatlantic accent, debonair demeanor and "dashing good looks," Grant is considered one of classic Hollywood's definitive leading men.

Grant was named the second Greatest Male Star of All Time after Humphrey Bogart by the American Film Institute. He was known for both comedic and dramatic roles; his best-known films includes *The Awful Truth* in 1937, *Bringing Up Baby* in 1938, *Gunga Din* in 1939, *The Philadelphia Story* in 1940, *His Girl Friday* in 1940, *Arsenic and Old Lace* in 1944, *Notorious* in 1946, *The Bishop's Wife* in 1947, *To Catch a Thief* in 1955, *An Affair to Remember* in 1957, *North by Northwest* in 1959 and *Charade* in 1963.

Nominated twice for the Academy Award for Best Actor in *Penny Serenade* and *None But the Lonely Heart* and five times for a Golden Globe Award for Best Actor, Grant was continually passed over. In 1970, he was presented an Honorary Oscar at the 42nd Academy Awards by Frank Sinatra "for his unique mastery of the art of screen acting with the respect and affection of his colleagues."

Cary Grant retired from the screen when he was 62 when his daughter was born, in order to focus on bringing her up and to provide a sense of permanency and stability in her life.[20]

CABLE ADDRESS UNFILMAN

UNIVERSAL PICTURES COMPANY, INC.
UNIVERSAL-INTERNATIONAL PICTURES
UNIVERSAL CITY, CALIFORNIA

August 16, 1962

Dr. M. J. Bagley, Director
Famous People's Eye Glasses Museum
61 East Frontier Blvd.
Henderson, Nevada

Dear Dr. Bagley:

These old eye glasses of mine
come to you in response to your recent letter
of request. I trust they will be a suitable
and welcome addition to your growing collection.

Sincerely,

Cary Grant

Enc.

ALFRED HITCHCOCK

Birth name	Alfred Joseph Hitchcock
Born	13 August 1899
	Leytonstone, Essex, England
Died:	29 April 1980 (aged 80)
Other Names:	Hitch, the Master of Suspense
Alma mater:	Salesian College, St Ignatius' College
Occupation:	Film director, Film producer
Years Active:	1921-1976
Influenced by:	Fitz Lang, Sergel Eisenstein, FW Murnau
Religion:	Roman Catholic
Spouse(s):	Alma Reville
Children:	Patricia Hitchcock

I am amazed that Alfred Hitchcock, at the age of 62, has not worn any eyeglasses after he has written a multitude of movies and television shows.

He pioneered many techniques in the suspense and psychological thriller genres. After a successful career in British cinema in both silent films and early talkies, billed as England's best director, Hitchcock moved to Hollywood in 1939.

He is the second son and youngest of three children of William Hitchcock, a greengrocer and poulterer, and

Emma Jane Whelan. He often described a lonely and sheltered childhood worsened by his obesity. It was interesting when he was 5 years old his father sent him to the local police station with a note asking the officer to lock him away for 5 minutes as punishment for behaving badly.

For over fifty years, Hitchcock fashioned for himself a distinctive and recognizable directorial style. He pioneered the use of a camera made to move in a way that mimics a person's gaze, forcing viewers to engage in a form of voyeurism and framed shots to maximize anxiety, fear, or empathy, and used innovative film editing. Many of Hitchcock's films have twist endings and thrilling plots featuring depictions of violence, murder, and crime. Many of the mysteries, are used as decoys or "MacGuffins" that serve the film's themes and the psychological examinations of the characters. Hitchcock's films also borrow many themes from psychoanalysis and feature strong sexual overtones. Through his cameo appearances in his own films, interviews, film trailers, and the television program *Alfred Hitchcock Presents,* he became a cultural icon.[21]

Melvin J. Bagley

ALFRED J. HITCHCOCK PRODUCTIONS, INC.
UNIVERSAL CITY, CALIF. • TRIANGLE 7-1211

August 20, 1962

Dr. M.J. Bagley
Famous People's Eye Glasses Museum
61 East Frontier Blvd.
Hnederson, Nevada

Dear Dr. Bagley:

Mr. Hitchcock has asked me to thank you for your letter requesting a pair of his eye glasses. Unfortunately, Mr. Hitchcock cannot contribute to your Museum as he has never worn glasses.

Thank you for your interest however.

Sincerely,

Suzanne Gauthier
Secretary to
Mr. Hitchcock

RICHARD RODGERS

Birth name:	Richard Charles Rodgers
Born:	June 28, 1902
	New York City, New York US
Died:	December 30, 1979 (aged 77)
	New York City, New York, US
Genres:	Musical theatre
Occupation:	Composer songwriter, playwright

> As time goes by, the music Mr. Rodgers composed with Hart and Hammerstein, makes him a true musical genius. As he promised his glasses now sit in my collection.

Richard Rodgers was an American composer of music for more than 900 songs and for 43 Broadway musicals. He also composed music for films and television. He is best known for his songwriting partnerships with the lyricists Lorenz Hart and Oscar Hammerstein II. His compositions have had a significant impact on popular music down to the present day, and have an enduring broad appeal.

Rodgers was the first person to win what are considered the top show business awards in television, recording, movies and Broadway—an Emmy, a Grammy, an Oscar, and a Tony—now known collectively as an EGOT. He has also won a Pulitzer Prize, making him one of two people, Marvin Hamlisch is the other, to receive each award.[22]

Richard Rodgers

488 MADISON AVENUE • NEW YORK 22, N. Y.

Telephone MUrray Hill 8-3640

August
23rd
1962

Dear Dr. Bagley:

At the moment the only eye glasses in my

possession are in use. However, my

secretary who is writing this reply for

me knows that when one of my eye glasses

becomes available, it is to be sent to

you for your collection. With thanks for

your interest, I am

Yours sincerely,

Richard Rodgers

Dr. M. J. Bagley
Director
Famous People's Eye Glasses Museum
61 East Frontier Boulevard
Henderson, Nevada

COLE PORTER

Born:	June 9, 1891
	Peru Indiana, US
Died:	October 15, 1964 (aged 73)
Cause of Death:	Kidney Failure
Occupation:	Composer and Songwriter
Spouse(s)	Linda Lee Thomas

Cole Porter was a very amazing person. He was one of the few composers that wrote the words and the music to all his songs. When he wrote the song *Love for Sale,* it was banned because it was not acceptable at his time when he wrote the song.

Cole Porter was born to a wealthy family in Indiana. His love for music defied the wishes of his domineering grandfather to become a lawyer. Classically trained, he was drawn towards musical theatre. After a slow start, he began to achieve success in the 1920s, and by the 1930s he was one of the major songwriters for the Broadway musical stage. Unlike many successful Broadway composers, Porter wrote the lyrics as well as the music, for his songs.

After a serious horseback riding accident in 1937, Porter was left disabled and in constant pain, but he continued to work. His shows of the early 1940s did not contain the lasting hits of his best work of the 1920s and 30s, but in 1948 he made a triumphant comeback with his most successful musical, *Kiss Me, Kate*. It won the first Tony Award for best musical.

Porter's other musicals include *Fifty Million Frenchmen, DuBarry Was a Lady, Anything Goes, Can-Can and Silk Stockings*. His numerous hit songs include; *Night and Day, I Get a Kick Out of You, Well, Did You Evah!, I've Got You Under My Skin, My Heart Belongs to Daddy,* and *You're the Top*. He also composed scores for films from the 1930s to the 1950s, including Born to Dance in 1936, which featured the songs *You'd Be So Easy to Love* and *I've Got You Under My Skin,* Rosalie in 1937, which featured *In the Still of the Night,* High Society in 1956, which included *True Love,* and Les Girls in 1957.

In 1917, Porter maintained a luxury apartment, where he entertained lavishly in Paris. His parties were extravagant and scandalous, with "much gay and bisexual activity, Italian nobility, cross-dressing, international musicians, and a large surplus of recreational drugs." In 1918, he met Linda Lee Thomas, a rich, Louisville, Kentucky-born divorcée eight years his senior. She was beautiful and well-connected socially, and the couple shared mutual interests, including a love of travel, and she became Porter's confidant and companion. The couple married the following year. She was in no doubt about Porter's homosexuality, but it was mutually advantageous for them to marry. It was a respectable heterosexual front in an era when homosexuality was not publicly acknowledged. They were genuinely devoted to each other and remained married from December 19, 1919, until her death in 1954.[23]

FROM: COLE PORTER

August 25, 1962

Dr. M. J. Bagley, Director
Famous People's Eye Glasses Museum
61 East Frontier Blvd.,
Henderson, Nevada

Dear Dr. Bagley:

    Under separate cover I am
sending you the pair of eye glasses
you requested. I still use this
type of frame for my glasses.

    It was nice of you to write to
me and I wish you much success with
your collection.

           Sincerely,

           Cole Porter

CP:te

EMILY POST

Birth name	Emily Price
Born	October 27, 1872
	Baltimore, Maryland, US
Died:	September 25, 1960 (aged 87)
	New York City, New York. US
Occupation:	Author, Founder of the Emily Post Institute
Nationality:	American
Education:	Finishing School
Subjects:	Etiquette
Spouse(s)	Edwin Main Post (1892-1905)
Children:	Edwin Main Post Jr., Bruce Price Post
Relative(s):	Elizabeth Post, Peggy Post, Bruce Price

When I was a kid my mother was a great teacher and believer of good table manners. Emily Post was my mother's model for teaching us good manners which I have all my life been a strong believer in.

Emily Post was an American author for writing on etiquette.

Post was born as Emily Price, her father the architect, Bruce Price and her mother was Josephine Lee of Wilkes-Pennsylvania. After being educated at home in her early years, she attended Graham's finishing school in New York, after her family moved there.

Price met her future husband, Edwin Main Post, a prominent banker, at a ball in a Fifth Avenue mansion. Following their wedding in 1892 and a honeymoon tour, they lived in New York's Washington Square. They also had a country cottage named Emily Post Cottage in Tuxedo Park, which was one of four Bruce Price Cottages that she inherited from her father, Bruce Price.

The couple divorced in 1905, because her husband's affairs with chorus girls and fledgling actresses, which had made him the target of blackmail.

When Post's two sons were old enough to attend boarding school, Post began to write. She began to write for the newspapers and magazines about architecture and interior design. She also wrote books such as *Flight of a Moth* in 1904, *Purple and Fine Linen* in 1906, *Woven in the Tapestry* in 1908, *The Title Market* in 1909, and *The Eagle's Feather* in 1910.

In 1922 her book *Etiquette in Society, in Business, in Politics and at Home* became the best seller, and updated versions continued to be popular for decades.

In 1946, she founded The Emily Post Institute, which continues her work. Peggy Post, wife of Emily's great-grandson, is the current spokeswoman for The Emily Post Institute and writes etiquette advice for *Good Housekeeping* magazine, succeeding her mother in law, Elizabeth Post. She is the author of more than twelve books.[24]

EMILY POST INSTITUTE, Inc.

August 27, 1962

Dear Dr. Bagley,

We are very sorry not
to be able to comply with your
request but Mrs. Post passed
away about a year and a half
ago and all of her possessions
were disposed of at that time.

Very sincerely,

Isabel Paul

HELENA RUBINSTEIN

Birth name	Chaya Rubinstein
Born	December 25, 1870
	Krakow, Austria-Hungary (modern-day-Poland)
Died:	April 1, 1965 (aged 94)
Marriage:	Edward William Titus
Children:	Roy Valentine Titus and Horace Titus

Helena Rubinstein was a Polish-born American business magnate. Helena was the eldest daughter of eight. Her parents are Augusta Gitte Shaindel and Horace Naftoli Hertz Rubinstein, a shopkeeper in Krakow.

Rubinstein at 32, arrived in Australia with no money and little English. Her stylish clothes and milky complexion did not pass unnoticed among the town's ladies, however, and she soon found enthusiastic buyers for the jars of beauty cream made of lanolin in her luggage. Later on she began to make her own beauty cream. She was the founder and eponym of Helena Rubinstein, Incorporated, which made her one of the world's richest women. Thirteen years later she and Titus moved to New York City, where she opened a cosmetics salon. Elizabeth Aden and Rubinstein were vicious rivals, both aware of effective marketing and luxurious packaging, the value of celebrity endorsement, attractive beauticians in neat uniforms, the perception of the value of overpricing and the promotion of the pseudo-science of skincare.

A multimillionaire of contrasts, Rubinstein took a bag lunch to work and was very frugal in many matters, but bought top fashion clothing and valuable fine art and furniture.[25]

Helena Rubinstein
655 Fifth Avenue
New York 22. N.Y

August 30th, 1962

Dr. M. J. Bagley, Director
Famous People's Eye Glasses Museum
61 East Frontier Boulevard
Henderson, Nevada

Dear Mr. Bagley,

Thank you for your letter of August 16th, addressed to Madame Rubinstein, requesting a pair of her old eye glasses for your Museum.

Unfortunately, Madame Rubinstein is traveling through Europe at the present time. Even if she were here in the States, however, I doubt if we could help you, because to my knowledge, Madame Rubinstein does not have any old eye glasses in her possession.

On Madame Rubinstein's behalf, all good wishes to you.

Sincerely yours,

Nancy Levey
Executive Secretary to
Madame Helena Rubinstein

LAWRENCE WELK

Born:	March 11, 1903
	Strasburg, North Dakota
Died:	May 17, 1992 (aged 89)
	Santa Monica, California
Occupation:	Musician, accordionist, bandleader, and television impresario
Religion:	Roman Catholic
Spouse(s)	Fern Veronica Rener (1931-1992) (his death)
Children:	Shirley Welk, Donna Welk, Lawrence "Larry" Welk, Jr.
Website:	Welk Musical Family (http://www.welkshow.org/)

> I was never a fan of Lawrence Welk. He was a great advocate of simplicity, but because of this simplicity, millions of people that love music written and played like he did, loved his style.

Lawrence Welk was an American musician, accordionist, bandleader, and television impresario, who hosted *The Lawrence Welk Show* from 1955 to 1982. His style came to be known to his large number of radio, television, and live-performance fans and critics as "champagne music."

In 1996, Welk was ranked #43 on TV Guide's 50 Greatest TV Stars of All Time.

Welk was married for 61 years, until his death, to Fern Renner, with whom he had three children.

Known as an excellent businessman, Welk had investments in real estate and music publishing. Welk was the general partner in a commercial real estate development located at 100 Wilshire Boulevard in Santa Monica, California. The 21-story tall white tower is the tallest building in Santa Monica and is located on the bluffs overlooking Santa Monica Bay. It was informally named "The Lawrence Welk Champagne Tower."

Welk enjoyed playing golf which he first took up in the late 1950s and was often a regular at many celebrity pro-ams such as the Bob Hope Desert Classic.

A devout lifelong Roman Catholic, Welk was a daily communicant, which is corroborated in numerous biographies, by his autobiography and by his family and his many staff, friends and associates throughout the years.

Welk died from pneumonia in Santa Monica, California in 1992 at age 89 and was buried in Culver City's Holy Cross Cemetery.[26]

THE CHAMPAGNE MUSIC OF

LAWRENCE WELK

September 10, 1962

Dr. M. J. Bagley
Famous People's Eye Glasses Museum
61 East Frontier Blvd.
Henderson, Nev.

Dear Dr. Bagley:

I received your letter and am sorry to say that
I do not have any old eye glasses on hand at this
time. I always throw the old ones away as soon
as I get new ones, however, I will keep your letter on hand in the event that I get a new pair in
the near future.

Sincerely yours,

Lawrence Welk
LW:ll

Melvin J. Bagley

THE CHAMPAGNE MUSIC OF

LAWRENCE WELK

June 16, 1965

Dear Dr. Bagley:

I received your letter and thank you for your interest in adding a pair of my glasses to the Famous People's Eye Glasses Museum.

I just purchased new glasses but, unfortunately, as in the past, I gave my old glasses to our church who collects them for old folks' homes. For that reason, I do not have any old ones on hand to send.

Kindest regards.

Sincerely,

Lawrence Welk
LW:ll

ABC-TV NETWORK · SATURDAY EVENINGS · 8:30 TO 9:30 P.M. (ET)

ANN SOTHERN

Birth name	Harriette Arlene Lake
Born	January 22, 1909
	Valley City, North Dakota US
Died:	March 15, 2001 (aged 92)
	Ketchum, Idaho, US
Cause of Death:	Heart failure
Resting Place:	Ketchum Cemetery
Nationality:	American
Other names:	Harriet Byron, Harriet Lake
Education:	Minneapolis Central High School
	Alma materUniversity of Washington
Occupation:	Actress, Singer
Years active:	1927-1987
Spouses:	Roger Pryor, Robert Sterling
Children:	Patricia Ann Sterling

When I received letters like this, I felt the person writing the letter had good intentions. I was always happy to get a letter on their behalf.

Ann Sothern was an American stage, radio, film and television actress. Sothern began her career in the late 1920s in bit parts in films. In 1930, she made her Broadway stage debut. In 1939, MGM cast her as Maisie Ravier, a brash yet loveable Brooklyn showgirl. The character proved to be popular and spawned a successful film series and radio show, *The Adventures of Maisie.*

In 1953, Sothern moved into television as the star of her own sitcom *Private Secretary.* The series aired for five seasons on CBS and earned Sothern three Primetime Emmy Award nominations. In 1958, she starred in another sitcom for CBS, *The Ann Sothern Show* aired for three seasons. From 1965 to 1966, Sothern provided the voice of Gladys Crabtree in the sitcom *My Mother the Car.* She continued her career throughout the late 1960s with stage and film appearances and guest starring roles on television. Due to health issues, she worked sporadically during the 1970s and 1980s.

In 1987, Sothern appeared in her final film *The "Whales of August,"* starring Bette Davis and Lillian Gish. Sothern earned her first and only Academy Award nomination for Best Supporting Actress for her role in the film. After filming concluded, she retired to Ketchum, Idaho where she spent her remaining years before her death from heart failure in March 2001.

Ann Sothem has two stars on the Hollywood Walk of Fame, for the motion pictures located at 1612 Vine Street, and television located at 1634 Vine Street.[27]

Ann Sothern

Famous Peoples Eyeglasses Museum
61 East Frontier Blvd.,
Henderson, Nevada

                    Attention: Dr. M.J. Bagley, Dir.

Dear Dr. Bagley:

I am writing in answer to your letter of August 17th to
Miss Ann Sothern.

Miss Sothern has just returned from Europe, and has
not had time to get to her mail.

I shall see that your letter reaches Miss Sothern's attention, and if possible, we will try to find a pair of eyeglasses to send to you.

With every good wish, and may we thank you for your
interest.

Harriet Flanegin
Sec'y. to Miss Sothern

September 11, 1962

PEGGY LEE

Birth name	Norma Deloris Egstrom
Born:	May 26, 1920
	Jamestown, North Dakota
Died:	January 21, 2002 (aged 81)
	Belair, Los Angeles, California
Genres:	Traditional pop, jazz
Occupations:	Singer, actress, songwriter
Years Active:	1941-2000
Labels:	Decca Records
	Capital Records
Marriage:	Dave Barbour, Brad Dexter, Dewey Martin, Jack Del Rosario
Child:	Nicki Lee Foster

Do you remember the song *Nice Work?* Nobody can sing this song like Peggy Lee.

Peggy Lee was an American jazz and popular music singer, songwriter, composer and actress. She wrote music for films, acted, and created conceptual record albums encompassing poetry, jazz, chamber pop, and art songs.

Lee's mother died when she was four years old. Her father married Min Schaumber, who treated her with great great cruelty while her alcoholic father did little to stop it. As a result , she developed her musical talent and took several part-time jobs so that she could be away from home. Lee first sang professionally over KOVC radio in Valley City, North Dakota. She later had her own series on a radio show sponsored by a local restaurant that paid her in food. At 17 she left home and went to Los Angeles.

When she was 23, she married Dave Barbour who was a guitarist in Benny Goodman's band. They had a daughter Nicki. She was going to retire and raise their daughter, but after a while she went back to song writing and singing.

Peggy Lee is internationally recognized for her signature song "Fever."

In her 60 year long career, Peggy was the recipient of three Grammy Awards including a Lifetime Achievement Award, and an Academy award nomination, the American Society of Composers, Authors and Publishers Award, the President's Award, the Ella Award for Lifetime Achievement, and the Living Legacy Award from the Woman's international Center. In 1999 Peggy Lee was inducted into the Songwriter's Hall of Fame.

Lee continued to perform into the 1990s, sometimes in a wheelchair. After years of poor health, Lee died of complications form diabetes and a heart attack at age 81. She was buried in Westwood Village Memorial Park Cemetery in Los Angeles. On her marker in a garden setting is inscribed, "Music is my life's breath.[28]

September 13, 1962

Dr. M. J. Bagley
Director
Famous Peoples' Eye Glasses Museum
61 East Frontier Boulevard
Henderson, Nevada

Dear Dr. Bagley,

What an interesting idea to collect eye glasses!
Although I do not wear prescription glasses, perhaps you might like a pair of sunglasses? The
pair I am sending you are mine and have been worn
by me.

I would like to extend my good wishes for the
success of your project.

Sincerely,

pl/bj

DEAN RUSK

Birth name:	David Dean Rusk
Born:	February 9, 1909
	Cherokee County, Georgia
Died:	December 20, 1994 (aged 85)
	Athens, Georgia
	Political PartyDemocratic
Alma mater:	Davidson College
	Oxford University
	University of California–Berkeley
Profession:	Professor, Soldier, Politician
Marriage:	Virginia Foisie they have 3 children
	United States, Secretary of State
In office:	January 21, 1961-January 20, 1969
President:	John F. Kennedy
	Lyndon B Johnson
	2nd Assistant Secretary of State for far Eastern Affairs
In Office:	March 28, 1950–December 9, 1951
President:	Harry S. Truman
	1st Assistant Secretary of State for International Organization Affairs
In Office:	February 8, 1949-May 26, 1949
President:	Harry S. Truman

David Dean Rusk was the joint-second-longest serving US Secretary of State of all time, behind only Cordell Hull and tied with William H. Seward.

His parents are Robert Hugh and Frances Elizabeth Clotfelter Rusk. While studying in England as a Rhodes Scholar at St. John's College, Oxford, he received the Cecil Peace Prize in 1933.

He taught at Mills College in Oakland, California from 1934 to 1949 and earned a law degree at the University of California, Berkeley in 1940.

During World War II he joined the infantry as a reserve captain, and served as a staff officer in the China Burma India Theater. At the end of the war he was a colonel, decorated with the legion of Merit with Oak Leaf Cluster.

He returned to America to work briefly for the war Department in Washington. He joined the department of state in 1945, and worked for the office of United Nations Affairs. He suggested splitting Korea into spheres of U.S. and of Soviet influence at the 38th parallel north.

Rusk received both the Sylvanus Thayer Award and the Presidential Medal of Freedom in 1969. Following his retirement, he taught international law at the University of Georgia School of Law in Athens, Georgia from 1970 to 1984.[29]

SPECIAL ASSISTANT TO THE SECRETARY OF STATE
WASHINGTON

September 17, 1962

Dear Dr. Bagley:

Thank you for your letter of August 16 to
Secretary Rusk. He regrets that he does not
have a pair of glasses to contribute to your
museum, but he appreciates your giving him the
opportunity to do so.

Sincerely yours,

Emory C. Swank

Dr. M. J. Bagley,
   Director, Famous People's Eye Glasses Museum,
      61 East Frontier Boulevard,
         Henderson, Nevada.

GARRY MOORE

Birth name:	Thomas Garrison Morfit, III
Born:	January 31, 1915
	Baltimore, Maryland US
Died:	November 28, 1993 (aged 78)
	Hilton Head, South Carolina, US
Cause of Death:	Emphysema
Occupation:	Entertainer, Game show host, Comedian
Years Active:	1949-1977
Spouse(s):	Eleanor "Nell" Borum Little
	Mary Elizabeth De Chant

Garry Moore was an American entertainer, game show host and comedian best known for his work in television. Born Thomas Garrison Morfit III, Moore entered show business as a radio personality in the 1940s and was a television host on several game and variety show programs for three decades.

After dropping out of high school, Moore found success as a radio host and then moved on to the television industry. He hosted *The Gary Moore Show,* and the game shows *I've Got a Secret* and *To Tell the Truth.* He became known for his bow ties and his crew cut.

From 1943 to 1947, Jimmy Durante and Garry Moore had a joint show, with Moore as the straight man.

Impressed with his ability to interact with audiences, CBS offered him his own show called *"The Garry Moore Show."* In 1964, he had worked on radio and television for 27 uninterrupted years. Moore decided to retire, saying he had "said everything he ever wanted to say three times already". After retiring he and his wife travelled around the world. In 1966, he went back to hosting *I've Got a Secret* and *To Tell The Truth.* By the time he retired he had worked 42 years.

After being diagnosed with throat cancer in 1976, Moore retired from the television industry, making a few rare television appearances.

He spent the last years of his life in South Carolina and at his summer home in Maine. Garry Moore died of emphysema at Hilton Head, South Carolina on November 28, 1993 at the age of 78.[30]

Melvin J. Bagley

THE GARRY MOORE SHOW
RED WING PRODUCTIONS, INC.

524 WEST 57th STREET · NEW YORK, NEW YORK · JUdson 6-6000

September 18, 1962

Dr. M.J. Bagley
Famous People's Eye Glasses Museum
61 East Frontier Boulevard
Henderson, Nevada

Dear Dr. Bagley:

Thank you for your kind offer to include a pair of
my eye glasses in the FAMOUS PEOPLE'S EYE GLASSES
MUSEUM. I'm flattered by this proposal, but I'm
afraid I don't wear glasses.

Again - thanks for thinking of me, and all good
wises.

Cordially,

GARRY MOORE

GM:fl

94

ULYSSES S. GRANT III

Born:	July 4, 1881, Chicago, Illinois
Died:	August 29, 1968 (aged 87), Clinton, Oneida County, New York
Allegiance:	United States of America
Service/Branch:	United States of America
Years of Service:	1903-1946
Rank:	Major General
Commands:	1st Engineer Regiment Engineer Replacement Training Center
	Office of Civilian Defense
Battles/wars:	Philippine American War, World War I, World War II
Award:	Distinguished Service Medal, Legion of Merit, Legion d'honneur Croix de guerre
Relations:	Ulysses S. Grant (grandfather)
	Frederick Dent Grant (father)
Spouse:	Edith Root
Children:	Edith, Clara Frances, and Julia
Other work:	Vice President of George Washington University

When I hear the word U.S. Grant, my belief is that he was the main driver in winning the civil war. I feel greatly honored to have his grandson's

glasses in my museum. His writing the letter
directly to me made it even more important.

Ulysses Simpson Grant III was an American soldier
and planner. Grant was born in Chicago and educated
in Austria, where his father was the U.S. diplomat. He
attended Columbia University until 1898 when he
received an appointment to West Point.

Grant was assigned to the Corps of Engineers of the
United States Army. He also served in the General Staff
Corps from 1917 to 1920 and 1936 to 1940.

Grant served on Mindanao, Philippines in 1903
to 1904, the Cuban Pacification in 1906, the Mexican
Border Service in 1912 to 1917, including the Veracruz
Expedition in 1914 and the Pancho Villa Expedition in
1916 in World War I and World War II.

In 1940, Grant was Division Engineer for the Great
Lakes in Cleveland, Ohio. He was promoted to Brigadier
General. In 1943, Grant was promoted to Major General.

After the war, Grant retired from the Army. He served
on the National Capital Park and Planning Commission,
and was Vice President of the George Washington
University from 1946 to 1951. He served as President of
the American Planning and Civic Association from 1947
to 1949, and the National Council of Historic Sites and
a trustee of the National Trust for Historic Preservation.
Grant's testimony as a Corps of Engineers veteran
before Congress in opposition to the Echo Park Dam in
Dinosaur National Monument was a key element in the
cancellation of the project, and in protection of National
Park lands against water development projects.

Grant was chairman of the Civil War Centennial Commission from 1957 to 1961. He resigned from the commission due to the illness of his wife.[31]

U. S. GRANT 3RD, MAJ. GEN. U.S.A. RET.
1135 TWENTY-FIRST STREET, N. W.
WASHINGTON 6, D. C.

September 21, 1962

Dr. M. J. Bagley, Director
Famous People's Eye Glasses Museum
61 East Frontier Boulevard
Henderson, Nevada

My dear Dr. Bagley:

Matters of great urgency have prevented my replying to your letter of July 5th until now.

I regret that I have no eye glasses of my Grandfather's to give your museum.

As to a pair of mine, although I do not consider that they rate a place in your museum, I will send you a pair as soon as I can find some not in use.

Sincerely yours

U. S. GRANT 3rd

JACK LEMMON

Birth name:	John Uhler Lemmon
Born:	February 8, 1925
	Newton, Massachusetts, U S
Died:	June 27, 2001 (aged 76)
	Los Angeles. California, U S
Cause of Death:	Colon cancer, Bladder cancer
Resting Place:	Westwood Village Memorial Park Cemetery
Education:	Phillips Academy
Alma mater:	Harvard University
Occupation:	Actor
Years active:	1949-2000
Spouse:	Cynthia Stone, Felicia Farr
Children:	Courtney and stepdaughter Denise
Religion:	Catholic

Some Like It Hot, The Apartment, Mister Roberts, Days of Wine and Roses, Great Race, Irma la Douce, The Odd Couple, Save the Tiger, The Out-of-Towners, The China Syndrome, Missing, Glengarry Glen Ross, Grumpy Old Men, Grumpier Old Men, The Odd Couple II are some of Jack Lemmon's notable films.

I am always very touched when I look at the letters in my museum and see how some of the great people that have lived the same time I did, have passed on.

Jack Lemmon was born in an elevator at Newton-Wellesley Hospital in Newton, Massachusetts. He was the only son of John Uhler Lemmon Jr., president of a doughnut company and Mildred Burgess LaRue Noel. When he was 8, he knew he wanted to be an actor. John Uhler "Jack" Lemmon III was an American actor and musician. He starred in more than 60 films, including: "Some Like it Hot", "The Apartment, Mister Roberts" (for which he won the 1955 Best Supporting Actor Academy Award), "Days of Wine and Roses," "The Great Race," "Irma La Douce," " The Odd Couple, Save the Tiger"(for which he won the 1973 Best Actor Academy Award). "The Out-of-Towners," "The China Syndrome," "Missing" (for which he won Best Actor at the 1982 Cannes Film Festival), Glengarty Glen Ross, "Grumpy Old Men" and "Grumpier Old Men."

In the late 1960s, Jack Lemmon admitted that he was an alcoholic.

Jack Lemmon died of colon cancer and metastatic cancer of the bladder on June 27, 2001. He had been fighting the disease, very privately, for two years before he died.[32]

Sept. 23rd '62

JACK LEMMON

Dear Dr. Bagley-

Mr. Lemmon asked me to answer your letter of July 26th — Am sorry to be so late - but Mr. Lemmon just returned from Europe. He is very sorry he has no eyeglasses to send you - as he doesn't wear eye glasses - maybe some future time.

Sincerely

Jack Lemmon

per. m.n.s. social sec'y

ERLE STANLEY GARDNER

Born:	July 17, 1889
	Malden, Massachusetts, US
Died:	March 11, 1970 (aged 80)
	Temecula, California, US
Pen name:	Kyle Corning, A.A Fair, Charles M. Green, Carleton Kendrake, Charles J. Kenny, Robert Parr, Les Tillray
Occupation:	Lawyer, writer
Education:	Palo Alto High School (1909) Valparaiso University School of Law (1 month)
Genres:	Detective Fiction, True Crime, Travel writing
Notable works:	Perry Mason, Cool and Lam, Doug Selby
Notable Award(s):	Grand Master Award, Mystery Writers of America, Edgar Award

When I received this letter from the gentleman who wrote the Perry Mason series, I was actually flattered that he would take the time to write the letter. Strangely enough I had a business dealing with his friend Murl Emery, who knew more about mining law than any attorney I could find.

Erle Stanley Gardner was an American lawyer and author of detective stories. Best known for the Perry Mason series, he also published under the pseudonyms A. A. Fair, Kyle Coming, Charles M. Green Carleton Kendrake, Charles J. Kenny, Les Tillray and Robert Parr.

He attended law school for approximately one month, was suspended from school when his interest in boxing became a distraction, then settled in California where he became a self-taught attorney and passed the state bar exam in 1911. He opened his own law office in Merced, California, than worked for five years for a sales agency. In 1921, he returned to the practice of law, creating the firm of Sheridan, Orr, Drapeau and Gardner in Ventura, California.

In 1912, he wed Natalie Frances Talbert; they had a daughter, Grace. Gardner practiced at the Ventura firm until 1933, when *The Case of the Velvet Claws* was published.

Gardner was bored by the routine of legal practice, the only part of which he enjoyed was trial work and the development of trial strategy. He wrote for Perry Mason in the 1930s and 1940s. Eventually Perry Mason became a long-running TV series with Raymond Burr as the title character.

Gardner gave up the practice of law to devote full-time to writing. In 1937 he moved to Temecula, California, where he lived for the rest of his life. In 1968 he married his long-time secretary Agnes Jean Bethell (1902–2002), the "Real Della Street."

Gardner died on March 11, 1970, in Temecula, California. His ashes were scattered over the Baja California Peninsula.[33]

ERLE STANLEY GARDNER
RANCHO DEL PAISANO
Temecula, California

September 28th, 1962

At Paradise, California

Dr. M. J. Bagley, Director
Famous People's Eye Glasses Museum
61 East Frontier Boulevard
Henderson, Nevada

Dear Dr. Bagley:

This is a greatly delayed answer to your letter of July 5th, because Mr. Gardner has been so busily engaged with his television and writing commitments that he hasn't had time to keep up with any except the most urgent correspondence.

Unfortunately, your letter happens to be one of a pattern. Mr. Gardner constantly receives letters from people who want some article which has been intimately associated with his life.

These requests have become so numerous that it is impossible to comply with them, and in instances where Mr. Gardner has complied with them, the results have sometimes been embarrassing.

You undoubtedly are well acquainted with Murl Emery, who is a close friend of Mr. Gardner's, and perhaps if you should run onto him on the street and can explain a little more about what you have in mind, what you intend to do with your collection when it is completed, etc., Mr. Emery could speak to Mr. Gardner personally.

Actually, at the moment, he doesn't have any "old glasses," because on his various trips to Mexico he has given away many of these glasses that he has outgrown, and while they undoubtedly were not closely adjusted to the eyes of persons who received the gifts, they were so much better than no glasses at all that they were very grateful.

Sincerely yours,

Secretary

MEL ALLEN

Born:	February 14, 1913
	Birmingham, Alabama
Died:	June 16, 1996 (aged 83)
Nationality:	American
Alma Mater:	University of Alabama
Occupation:	American Sportscaster

Mel Allen was an American sportscaster, best known for his long tenure as the primary play-by-play announcer for the New York Yankees. For three decades, Allen was arguably the most prominent member of his profession, his voice familiar to millions. Years after his death, he is still promoted as having been the "Voice of the New York Yankees." In his later years, he gained a second professional life as the first host of *This Week in Baseball*.

He was born Melvin Allen Israel in Birmingham, Alabama. During his time at Alabama, Israel served as the public address announcer for Alabama home football games. In 1933, when the station manager or sports director of Birmingham's radio station WBRC asked Alabama coach Frank Thomas to recommend a new play by play announcer, he suggested the 20 year old Israel. His first broadcast was Alabama's home opener that year, against Tulene.

Soon after graduating from Alabama University law school in 1937, Allen took a train to New York City for a weeks vacation. As it turned out, that one week stretched out to 60 years, he settled in New York and lived in the New York metropolitan area for the rest of his life.

The National Sportscasters and Sportswriters Association inducted Allen into its Hall of Fame in 1972. In 1978, he was one of the first two winners of the Baseball Hall of Fame's Ford C. Frick Award for broadcasting. In 1985, Allen was inducted into the American Sportscasters association Hall of Fame along with former Yankee partner Curt Gowdy and Chicago legend Jack Brickhouse. He was inducted into the National Radio Hall of fame in 1988.

Allen died of heart failure at the age of 83. He was buried at temple Bethel Cemetery in Stamford, Connecticut. On July 25, 1998, the Yankees dedicated a plaque in his memory for Monument Park at Yankee Stadium. The plaque calls him "A Yankee institution, a national treasure" and includes his much-spoken line, "How about that?!"[34]

NATIONAL BROADCASTING COMPANY, INC.

A SERVICE OF RADIO CORPORATION OF AMERICA

RCA Building, Radio City, New York 20, N.Y.

CIRCLE 7-8300

October 24, 1962

Dr. M. J. Bagley, Director
Famous People's Eye Glasses Museum
61 East Frontier Blvd.
Henderson, Nevada

Dear Dr. Bagley:

Mel Allen is out of town on a
football assignment but just before he left
he went through his mail and asked me to drop
you this line.

He thanks you very much for your
flattering request but regrets he cannot comply
since he does not wear glasses.

Sincerely yours,

Tillie Albagli
Secretary to Mel Allen

ta

PAT BOONE

Birth name:	Charles Eugene Boone
Born:	BornJune 1, 1934
	Jacksonville, Florida, US
Origin:	Nashville, Tennessee
Genres:	Christian, pop, country, rock and roll, patriotic.
Occupations:	Singer, songwriter, actor, motivational speaker, spokesman
Instruments:	Vocals, banjo, ukulele
Years Active:	1954 – present
Labels:	Republic, Dot, Tetragrammatons', Melodyland (Motown)
	Hip-O, The Gold Label, MCA

What I remember about Pat Boone was what a great comeback he made when he changed his style to gospel singing.

Charles Eugene "Pat" Boone is an American singer, actor, and writer. He was a successful pop singer in the United States during the 1950s and early 1960s. His hit songs were cover versions of black R&B artists' hit songs, when parts of the country were racially segregated and black musical artists were not played on white radio stations. He sold over 45 million albums, had 38 top 40 hits and appeared in more than 12 Hollywood movies.

According to Billboard, Boone was the second biggest charting artist of the late 1950s, behind only Elvis Presley, but ahead of Ricky Nelson and The Platters, and was ranked at No. 9, behind The Rolling Stones and Paul McCartney, but ahead of artists such as Aretha Franklin and The Beach Boys-in its listing of the Top 100 Top 40 Artists 1955–1995. Boone still holds the Billboard record for spending 220 consecutive weeks on the charts with one or more songs each week.

At the age of twenty-three, he began hosting a half-hour ABC variety television series, *The Pat Boone Chevy Showroom,* which aired for 115 episodes from 1957 to 1960. Many musical performers, including Edie Adams, Andy Williams, Pearl Bailey and Johnny Mathis made appearances on the show. His cover versions of rhythm and blues hits had a noticeable effect on the development of the broad popularity of rock and roll. During his tours in the 1950s, Elvis Presley was one of his opening acts.

As a prolific author, Boone had a No. 1 bestseller in the 1950s *Twixt Twelve and Twenty,* Prentice-Hall. In the 1960s, he focused on gospel music and is a member of the Gospel Music Hall of Fame. He continues to perform, and speak as a motivational speaker, a television personality, and a conservative political commentator.[35]

9033 WILSHIRE BOULEVARD, BEVERLY HILLS, CALIF,

PAT BOONE

TELEPHONE: CRESTVIEW 4-0751

November 1, 1962

Dr. M. J. Bagley
Famous People's Eye Glasses Museum
61 East Frontier Boulevard
Henderson, Nevada

Dear Dr. Bagley:

Thank you very much for your recent letter
to Pat Boone which has been brought to my
attention.

We wish we could help you, but unfortunately,
Mr. Boone has never had the need to wear
eye glasses (other than sun glasses) and,
therefore, we are unable to contribute a
pair of his old glasses for your museum.

Thank you for your interest in Mr. Boone which
he appreciates very much. All good wishes to
you with your museum project.

Sincerely,

Carol Coogan
Pat Boone Office

TIME & LIFE BLDG., ROCKEFELLER CENTER, NEW YORK 20, N. Y. PLAZA 7-4877

CAROL BURNETT

Birth name:	Carol Creighton Burnett
Born:	April 26, 1933
	San Antonio, Texas, US
Occupation:	Actress, comedian, singer, dancer, writer
Years active:	1955-present
Spouse(s):	Don Saroyan (m. 1955-1962)
	Joe Hamilton (m. 1963-1984)
	Brian Miller (m. 2001)
Children:	Carrie, Jody and Erin Hamilton

Getting a letter from Carol Burnett made me feel good. Since she doesn't wear glasses, she was unable to send a pair.

Carol Creighton Burnett is an American actress, comedian, singer, and writer. She is best known for her long-running TV variety show, *The Carol Burnett Show*, for CBS. She received success on stage, television, and film in varying genres including dramatic and comedy roles.

After a difficult childhood in San Antonio with alcoholic parents, Burnett discovered acting and comedy in college. She performed in nightclubs in New York City and had a breakout success on Broadway in 1959 in "Once Upon a Mattress," receiving a Tony Award nomination. She regularly appeared on *The Garry Moore Show* for the next three years, and winning her first Emmy Award in 1962. Burnett moved to Los Angeles and worked for 11 years on *The Carol Burnett Show* which aired on CBS television from 1967 to 1978. It was a variety show that combined comedy sketches, song and dance. Burnett created many memorable characters during the show's television run, and the show and her won numerous Emmy and Golden Globe Awards.

Burnett appeared in many television and film projects. Her film roles include *Pete 'n' Tillie* in 1972, *The Four Seasons* in 1981, *Annie* in 1982, *Noises Off* in 1992, and *Horton Hears a Who!* in 2008. She has appeared in other sketch shows; in dramatic roles in *6 Rms Riv Vu* in 1974 and *Friendly Fire* in 1979, in various well-regarded guest roles, such as in *Mad About You*, for which she won an Emmy Award; and in specials with Julie Andrews, Dolly Parton, Beverly Sills, and others. She was also back on Broadway in 1995 in *"Moon Over Buffalo,"* for which she was nominated for a Tony Award.[36]

Carol Burnett

November 8, 1962

Dr. M.J. Bagley, Director
Famous People's Eye Glasses Museum
61 East Frontier Boulevard
Henderson, Nevada

Dear Dr. Bagley:

Thank you for inviting me to send a
pair of eye glasses to your museum.
As I never have worn eye glasses, however,
I'm afraid I'm unable to add any to the
collection.

Thank you for thinking of me and all the
best of luck to you!

                    Sincerely,

                    Carol Burnett

CB/lm   Carol Burnett

NOEL COWARD

Birth name:	Sir Noel Peirce Coward
Born:	December 16, 1899
	Teddington, London
Died:	March 26, 1973
Occupation:	English Playwright, Composer, Director, Actor, Singer

> Sometimes when I wrote letters, the people I least expected to send glasses, were the ones who sent them. The only thing I remembered about Noel Coward was at one of interviews he did he said he did believe in the here after. He said there once was a dog who's name was Rover. When he was dead, he was dead all over.

Sir Noel Peirce Coward was an English playwright, composer, director, actor and singer, known for his wit, flamboyance, and he was what Time magazine called "a sense of personal style, a combination of cheek and chic, pose and poise."

Coward attended a dance academy in London, at the age of eleven, making his professional stage debut. As a teenager he was introduced into the high society in which most of his plays would be set. Coward published more than 50 plays from his teens. Many of his works, such as "Hay Fever," "Private Lives," "Design for Living," "Present Laughter and Blithe Spirit," have remained in the regular theatre repertoire. He composed hundreds of songs, in addition to well over a dozen musical theatre works including the operetta "Bitter Sweet" and comic revues, poetry, several volumes of short stories, the novel "Pomp and Circumstance," and a three-volume autobiography. Coward's stage and film acting and directing career spanned six decades, during which he starred in many of his own works.

During World War II, Coward volunteered to running the British propaganda office in Paris. He worked with the Secret Service, seeking to use his influence to persuade the American public and government to help Britain. Coward won an Academy Honorary Award in 1943 for his naval film drama, and was knighted in 1969. In the 1950s he achieved fresh success as a cabaret performing his own songs, such as "Mad Dogs and Englishmen," "London Pride," and "I Went to a Marvelous Party."

His plays and songs achieved new popularity in the 1960s and 1970s, and his work and style continue to influence popular culture. The former Albery Theatre originally the New Theatre in London was renamed the Noel Coward Theatre in his honor in 2006. By the end of the 1960s, he received a Tony Award for lifetime achievement.

Coward was homosexual but following the convention of his times, this was never mentioned. Coward firmly believed his private business was not for public discussion, considering "any sexual activities when over advertised" to be tasteless.

Coward died at his home in Firefly Estate in Jamaica of heart failure.[37]

NOËL COWARD

Les Avants,
sur Montreux,
Switzerland.

26th November 1962.

Dear Doctor Bagley,

I have much pleasure in sending you a pair of my glasses for your collection.

I used them for many years – they were my reading glasses – up until a few months ago when they had to be replaced by slightly stronger ones.

With all my good wishes for the continued success of your museum.

Yours sincerely,

JIMMY DOOLITTLE

Name:	James Harold "Jimmy" Doolittle
Born:	December14, 1896, Alameda, California
Died:	September 27, 1993 (aged 96), Pebble Beach, California
Place of burial:	Arlington National Cemetery
Allegiance:	U. S. of America, U. S. Air Forces, U. S. Army Air Forces,
	U. S. Army Air Corps, U S Army Air Service, Aviation Section, U.S. Signal Corps
	Years of Service:1917-1959
Rank:	General, Doctor
Commands held:	Twelfth Air Force, Fifteenth Air Force, Eighth Air Force
Battles/wars:	Mexican Border Service, World War I (Stateside Duty)
	World War II, Pacific Campaign, Doolittle Raid
	Mediterranean Campaign, European Campaign
	Cold War, Korean War (Stateside Duty)
Awards:	Medal of Honor, Distinguished Service Medal (2)
	Silver Star, Distinguished Flying Cross (3), Air Medal (4)
Other Work:	Shell Oil, VP, Director, Space Technology Laboratories, Chairman

When I first wrote to General Doolittle asking him for a glasses, I received a reply that he could not send a pair because they were still in use. Then a short time later, his glasses fell on the floor and broke. Although it was unfortunate for him, I was elated and very fortunate to get a pair of glasses from him.

General and Doctor Jimmy Doolittle, USAF was an American aviation pioneer. Doolittle served as an officer in the United States Army Air Forces during World War II. He earned the Medal of Honor for his valor and leadership as commander of the Doolittle Raid while a Lieutenant Colonel.

Doolittle's most important contribution to aeronautical technology was the development of instrument flying. In 1929, he became the first pilot to take off and land in airplane using instruments alone, without a view outside the cockpit.

In 1930 he resigned his regular commission and was commissioned a major in the Air Reserve Corps. He then became the manager of the Aviation Department of Shell Oil Company, in which capacity he conducted numerous aviation test. Doolittle helped influence Shell Oil Company to produce the first quantities of 100 octane aviation gasoline. High Octane fuel was crucial to the high performance planes.

In 1942, the Doolittle Raid in Japan is viewed by historians as a major morale-building victory for the United States. It showed the Japanese that their homeland was vulnerable to air attack and forced them to withdraw several front-line fighter units from Pacific War Zones for homeland defense.

Jimmy Doolittle married Josephine Daniels in 1917 and together they have two sons, James Jr. and John. Jimmy Doolittle died at the age of 96 and is buried in Arlington National Cemetery in Virginia next to his wife.[38]

SPACE TECHNOLOGY LABORATORIES, INC.
A SUBSIDIARY OF THOMPSON RAMO WOOLDRIDGE INC.
ONE SPACE PARK · REDONDO BEACH, CALIFORNIA

29 November 1962

Dr. M. J. Bagley
Director
Famous People's Eye Glasses Museum
61 East Frontier Boulevard
Henderson, Nevada

Dear Dr. Bagley:

Have yours of the fifteenth requesting a pair of used glasses. Am flattered by your request and regret that I do not have on hand a pair of glasses that is not in use.

As my eyes have gradually lost adaptability, have used the old reading glasses for shaving, card playing, shooting, etc.

Should a pair become available at a later date, will endeavor to send them on.

Very sincerely,

J. H. Doolittle

SPACE TECHNOLOGY LABORATORIES, INC.
A SUBSIDIARY OF THOMPSON RAMO WOOLDRIDGE INC.
ONE SPACE PARK · REDONDO BEACH, CALIFORNIA

7 January 1963

Dr. M. J. Bagley
Director
Famous People's Eye Glasses Museum
61 East Frontier Boulevard
Henderson, Nevada

Dear Dr. Bagley:

Since writing you in November General Doolittle has acquired
a pair of glasses which he thought you might like to have.
They are the old reading glasses he mentioned using for shaving,
shooting, etc. During World War II they were his reading
glasses. Just last week the frame broke, the glasses fell to the
ground and one lens completely shattered. I am mailing these
glasses to you under separate cover with the hope that the surviving lens will reach you intact.

Sincerely,

Donna Loop

Secretary to J. H. Doolittle

BETTY FURNESS

Birth name:	Elizabeth Mary Furness,
Born:	January 3, 1916, New York City, New York, United States
Died:	April 2, 1994 (age 78), New York City
Occupation:	Second special assistant to the president for Consumer Affairs
In office:	May 1, 1967 to January 20, 1969
President:	Lyndon B. Johnson
Political Party:	Democratic
Spouse(s):	Leslie Midgley, Bud Ernest, Johnny Green

Elizabeth Mary Furness was an American actress, consumer advocate and current affairs commentator.

In 1948 Furness was performing in the television series *Studio One,* which was broadcast live. She filled in for an actor to promote Westinghouse products during the advertisement break and impressed the company with her easy and professional manner. They offered her a contract to promote their products and she subsequently became closely associated with them. One of television's most recognizable series of commercials had Furness opening wide a refrigerator door, intoning, "You can be sure ... if it's Westinghouse."

Furness was a regular panelist on *"What's My Line?"* in 1951. She appeared in a series of live mysteries on

ABC television under the weighty title *Your Kaiser Dealer Presents Kaiser-Frazer "Adventures in Mystery" Starring Betty Furness in "Byline"* which ran in November and December 1951, and again on ABC in syndication in the fall of 1957. The series was produced by the DuMont Television Network and ran on DuMont under the title *News Gal.*

In 1953 she appeared in her own daytime television series *Meet Betty Furness,* which was sponsored by Westinghouse; she remained a spokesperson for the company until 1960. She then attempted to move into a less commercialized role in television but found herself too closely associated with advertising to be taken seriously. During this time she worked on radio, and also on behalf of the Democratic Party.

Furness has two stars on the Hollywood Walk of Fame for her contribution to Motion Pictures and to television.[39]

BETTY FURNESS

December 12, 1962

Dear Dr. Bagley:

I am afraid I can't oblige you, as I wear my old eye glasses.

Sincerely,

AGATHA CHRISTIE

Birth name:	Agatha Mary Clarissa Miller
Born:	15 September 1890
	Torquay, Devon, England
Died:	12 January 1976 (aged 85)
	Wallingford, Oxfordshire, England
Pen Name:	Mary Westmacott
Occupation:	Novelist/Short story
	Writer/Playwright/Poet
	NationalityBritish
Genres:	Murder mystery, Thriller, Crime fiction,
	Detective, Romances
Literary movement:	Golden Age of Detective Fiction
Spouse(s)	Archibald Christie (1914-1928)
	Max Mallowan (1930-1976; her death)
Children:	Rosalind Hicks (1919-2004

When I got this letter and the glasses of Agatha Christie, I and all the people in my office, were very happy. Mainly because it was one of the first pairs and was from a very famous person.

Dame Agatha Mary Clarissa Christie was a British crime writer of novels, short stories, and plays. She also wrote six romances under the name Mary Westmacott, but she is best remembered for the 66 detective novels and more than 15 short story collections she wrote under her own name, most of which revolve around the investigations of such characters as Hercule Poirot, Miss Jane Marple and Tommy and Tuppence. She also wrote the world longest-running play *The Mousetrap*.

Born to a wealthy upper-middle-class family Torquay, Devon, Christie served in a hospital during the First World War before marrying and starting a family in London. Although initially unsuccessful at getting her work published in 1920, The Bodley Head Press published her novel *The Mysterious Affair at Styles*, featuring the character of Poirot. This launched her literary career.

According to the *Guinness Book of World Records*, Christie is the best-selling novelist of all time. Her novels have sold roughly 4 billion copies, and her estate claims that her works rank third, after those of William Shakespeare and the Bible, as the world's most widely published books. In 1971, she was made a Dame by Queen Elizabeth II at Buckingham Palace.

In 1955, Christie was the first recipient of the Mystery Writers of America's highest honor, the Grand Master Award, and in the same year *Witness for the Prosecution* was given an Edgar Award by the MWA for Best Play. Many of her books and short stories have been filmed, and many have been adapted for television, radio, video games and comics.[40]

Melvin J. Bagley

WALLINGFORD 2246.

WINTERBROOK HOUSE,
WALLINGFORD,
BERKS.

28 December 1962

Dear Dr Bagley,

In reply to your letter of 24
October I have now found a pair I no
longer wear, and I have much pleasure
in presenting them to the Famous
People's Eye Glasses Museum.

Yours sincerely,

Agatha Christie

AGATHA CHRISTIE.

Dr M.J.Bagley,
Director,
Famous People's Eye Glasses Museum,
61 East Frontier Boulevard,
Henderson,
Nevada.

WILLIAM O. DOUGLAS

Birth name:	William Orville Douglas
Born:	October 16, 1898
	Maine Township, Minnesota
Died:	January 19, 1980 (aged 81)
	Bethesda, Maryland
Resting place:	Arlington National Cemetery
Spouses:	Mildred Riddle (1923-1953 (divorced)
	Mercedes Hester Davidson (1954-1963) (divorced)
	Joan Martin (1963-1966) (divorced)
	Cathleen Hefferman (1966-1980)
Occupation:	Associate Justice of the Supreme Court of the United States
	In officeApril 15, 1939-November 12, 1975
Nominated by:	Franklin D. Roosevelt

When I hear the name William O. Douglas, I think of the Supreme Court. To attain the status of a member of this elite group, he must be a true American, admired by all.

William Orville Douglas served as an Associate Justice of the Supreme Court of the United States. His term, lasting 36 years and 209 days (1939–75), is the longest term in the history of the Supreme Court. He was the

79th person appointed and confirmed to the bench of that court. In 1975 *Time* magazine called Douglas "the most doctrinaire and committed civil libertarian ever to sit on the court."

Douglas was the son of an itinerant Scottish Presbyterian minister from Pictou County, Nova Scotia. When he was six years old his father died, William, like the rest of the Douglas family, worked odds jobs to earn extra money, and a college education appeared to be unaffordable. As the valedictorian, he did well enough to earn a scholarship to Whitman College in Walla Walla, Washington.

He worked various jobs while attending school; as waiter and janitor during the school year and at a cherry orchard in the summer. Picking cherries, inspired him to a legal career. "I worked among the very very poor, the migrant laborer, the Chicanos and the IWWs who I saw being shot by the police. I saw cruelty and hardness, and my impulse was to be a force in other developments in the law."

He worked to support himself to law school at the Columbia Law School. He graduated fifth in his class. He taught at Columbia Law School and Yale Law School. At Yale he became an expert on commercial litigation and bankruptcy and was identified with the legal realist movement, which pushed for an understanding of law based less on formalistic legal doctrines and more on the real-world effects.

In 1974, he suffered a debilitating stroke in the right hemisphere of his brain, which paralyzed his left leg. This lead to his retirement.[41]

Supreme Court of the United States
Washington 25, D. C.

CHAMBERS OF
JUSTICE WILLIAM O. DOUGLAS   January 2, 1963

Dear Dr. Bagley:

Your letter of November 15 has
been received.

I am sending under separate
cover a pair of my eye glasses
which for obvious reasons have long
since been set aside but were worn
by me for several years.

Yours faithfully,

W. O. Douglas

Dr. M. J. Bagley
Director
Famous People's Eye
    Glasses Museum
61 East Frontier Boulevard
Henderson, Nevada

WALTER CRONKITE

Birth name:	Walter Leland Cronkite, Jr.
Born:	November 4, 1916
	Saint Joseph, Missouri, U.S.
Died:	July 17, 2009 (aged 92)
	New York City, New York, U.S.
Cause of death:	Cerebrovascular disease
Nationality:	American
Other names:	Old Ironpants, Uncle Walter, King of the anchormen
Occupation:	Television and radio broadcaster, news anchor
Years active:	1935-2009
Notable credit(s):	CBS Evening News
Home town:	Kansas City, Missouri
Religion:	Episcopalian
Spouse(s):	Mary Elizabeth Cronkite (m.1940-2005) her death
Children:	Nancy Elizabeth Cronkite, Kathy Cronkite, Walter Cronkite III
Grandchildren:	Will Ikard, John Ikard, Peter Cronkite, and Walter Cronkite IV

When I received this letter I was sure I didn't
think I would receive any glasses from him, but
I was wrong. He kept his promise and after 8

years he send us his glasses. What a wonderful surprise!

Walter Leland Cronkite, Jr. was an American Broadcast Journalist, best known as anchorman for the CBS Evening News for 19 years from 1962 to1981. He was often cited as "The Most Trusted Man in America". He reported many events from 1937 to 1981, including bombings in World War II, the Nuremberg trials, combat in the Vietnam War, Watergate, the Iran Hostage Crisis, and the murders of President John F. Kennedy, civil rights pioneer Martin Luther King, Jr., and Beatles musician John Lennon.

He was also known for his extensive coverage of the U.S. space program, from Project Mercury to the Moon landings to the Space Shuttle. He was the only non-NASA recipient of a Moon-Rock Award. Cronkite is well known for his departing catchphrase "And that's the way it is".[42]

CBS NEWS

A Division of Columbia Broadcasting System, Inc.

485 MADISON AVENUE, NEW YORK 22, NEW YORK · PLAZA 1-2345

January 4, 1963

Dr. M. J. Bagley
Director
Famous People's Eye Glasses Museum
61 East Frontier Blvd.
Henderson, Nevada

Dear Dr. Bagley:

Thank you for inviting Mr. Cronkite to contribute a pair of his glasses to your imagina-
tive sounding Museum.

I'm sorry that he's currently out of stock
on old glasses, but we'll hold on to the
next pair that he replaces with you in mind.

Sincerely yours,

Faith Adams

for Walter Cronkite

HERB SHRINER

Birth name:	Herbert Arthur Shriner
Born:	May 29, 1918, Toledo, Ohio
Died:	April 23, 1970 (aged 51)
	Delray Beach, Florida
Nationally:	American
Occupation:	Humorist, radio personality, television host

Herb Shriner is no Mark Twain, but he was close. I thought it was interesting when he mentioned in his letter that he did eat a lot of carrots, which apparently he thought would keep his vision good enough so he would not need glasses. Research shows carrots are important in adapting your eyes from daylight to dark (cones and rods) but does not save you from needing glasses.

Herbert Arthur "Herb" Shriner was an American humorist, radio personality and television host. In 1940, Shriner was hired by NBC for occasional radio appearances, which led to a regular spot in 1942 and 1943 on the comedy-variety program *Camel Caravan*. During World War II, he served in a United States Army special services unit and performed for two years in USO shows for GIs in Europe. After the war, he appeared on a number of radio shows, including *The Philip Morris Follies of 1946* with Johnny Desmond and Margaret Whiting.

In 1947 he appeared in a Broadway musical review called *Inside U.S.A.* The performances were panned by critics, but Shriner's monologues made it a success and carried the show for over a year. Shriner hosted *Herb Shriner Time,* a CBS Radio weekday program.

Herb Shriner Time evolved into a short-lived, fifteen-minute television show. A half-hour version on ABC ran during the 1951–52 season. It was more of a showcase for Shriner's humor than a game show, much like "You Bet Your Life," which starred Groucho Marx. "Two for the Money" gave Shriner an opportunity to deliver short monologues and harmonica solos. Seventeen-year old Woody Allen wrote jokes for Shriner's shows.

Shriner and his wife, Eileen "Pixie" McDermott, moved with their children to Florida, returning each summer to Angola, Indiana. Shriner invested in real estate and collected vintage automobiles. He and his wife were killed in Delray Beach, Florida in 1970 in one of those cars, a Studebaker Avanti, when the brakes failed. Some of his collection can be seen in the Auburn Cord Duesenberg Automobile Museum in Auburn, Indiana. Shriner's children are a daughter, Indy, and twin sons, actor, comedian and director named Wil Shriner, and soap opera actor Kin Shriner.[43]

HERB SHRINER
135 East 54th Street
New York 22, N. Y.

February 26, 1963

Dr. M. J. Bagley
Director
Famous People's Eye Glasses Museum
61 E. Frontier Boulevard
Henderson, Nevada

Dear Dr. Bagley:

Sorry to take so long in acknowledging
your letter -- my engagements have kept
me so busy hopping from one part of the
country to another lately that my correspondence is suffering accordingly.

Actually I don't really wear glasses often
enough to accumulate any old ones. I've
been eating lots of carrots, though, so if
this helps get my vision back to where it
ought to be, I'll be happy to send you my
one and only pair of glasses.

Your collection sounds very interesting.
If my travels take me out your way, I shall
certainly try to see it.

Sincerely yours,

HERB SHRINER

HS:ag

CONRAD HILTON

Birth name:	Conrad Nicholson Hilton
Born:	December 25, 1887
	San Antonio, New Mexico
	Territory, US
Died:	January 3, 1979 (aged 91)
	Santa Monica, California
	United States of America
Nationality:	American
Occupation:	Hotelier
Spouse(s):	Mary Adelaide Barron, Zsa Zsa Gabor, Mary Frances Kelly
Children:	Conrad Nicholson "Nicky" Hilton Jr.
	William Barron Hilton
	Eric Michael Hilton
	Constance Francesca Hilton

Conrad Nicholson Hilton was an American Hotelier. He is well known for being the founder of the Hilton Hotels chain.

The most enduring influence to shape Hilton's philanthropic philosophy beyond that of his parents was the Roman Catholic Church and his sisters. He credited his mother with guiding him to prayer and the church whenever he was troubled or dismayed from the boyhood loss of a beloved pony to severe financial losses during the Great Depression. His mother continually reminded him that prayer was the best investment he would ever make.

At the height of the oil boom, he bought his first hotel, the 40-room Mobley Hotel in Cisco, Texas, in 1919, when a bank purchase fell through. The hotel did such brisk business that rooms changed hands as much as three times a day, and the dining room was converted into additional rooms to meet the demand. He went on to buy and build hotels throughout Texas, including the high rise Dallas Hilton, opened in 1925, the Abilene Hilton in 1927, Waco Hilton in 1928, and El Paso Hilton in 1930. He built his first hotel outside of Texas in 1939 in Albuquerque. The rest is history.

In 1979, Hilton died at age 91. The bulk of his estate was left to the Conrad N. Hilton Foundation, which was established in 1944.[44]

CONRAD N. HILTON, PRESIDENT

OFFICE OF THE PRESIDENT
9990 SANTA MONICA BLVD.
BEVERLY HILLS, CALIFORNIA

June 4, 1963

Dr. M. J. Bagley, Director
Famous People's Eye Glasses Museum
61 East Frontier Boulevard
Henderson, Nevada

Dear Dr. Bagley:

Your letter addressed to Mr. Hilton's residence
has been received during his absence from the
country.

He is at present on an extended trip around the
world for the opening of several new Hilton Hotels,
and his itinerary indicates that he will not return
to the United States until the middle of the summer.

Sincerely yours,

Carmen Ong

Secretary to
CONRAD N. HILTON

cc

OFFICE OF THE CHAIRMAN
9990 SANTA MONICA BOULEVARD
BEVERLY HILLS CALIFORNIA

May 12, 1965

Dr. M. J. Bagley, Director
Famous People's Eye Glasses Museum
61 East Frontier Boulevard
Henderson, Nevada

Dear Dr. Bagley:

Your letter of May seventh was received by
Mr. Hilton.

We have checked once again, and are sorry
to advise you that he does not have any
old glasses which we could send you at
this time.

With best wishes.

Sincerely yours,

Elise M. Lincoln

Administrative Assistant
to CONRAD N. HILTON

OMW:cc

ROBERT F. KENNEDY

United States Senator from New York from January 3, 1965 – June 6, 1968
64th United States Attorney General January 20, 1961-September 3, 1964
under President John F Kennedy and Lyndon B Johnson.

Birth name:	Robert Francis Kennedy
Born:	November 20, 1925, Brookline, Massachusetts
Died:	June 6, 1968 (aged 42), Los Angeles, California
Resting Place:	Arlington National Cemetery, Arlington, Virginia
Nationality:	American
Political Party:	Democratic
Spouse(s):	Ethel Skakel
Children:	Kathleen Hartington, Joseph Patrick III, Robert Frances, Jr.,
	David Anthony, Mary Courtney, Michael LeMoyne, Mary Kerry, Christopher George, Matthew Maxwell Taylor, Douglas Harriman, and Rory Elizabeth Katherine.

Robert F. Kennedy joined the ranks of people in this book who died. He is one of the only people, along with the President of Egypt, who was assassinated.

Robert Francis "Bobby" Kennedy also referred to by his initials RFK, was an American politician, a Democratic Senator from New York, and a noted civil-rights activist. An icon of modem American liberalism and a member of the Kennedy family, he was a younger brother of President John F. Kennedy, and he served as the President's Chief Adviser and U.S. Attorney General.

Kennedy continued to serve as the Attorney General under President Lyndon B. Johnson for nine months. There had long been bad blood between them, so in September 1964 Kennedy resigned to seek a U.S. Senate seat from New York, which he won in November. Within a few years he publicly split with Johnson over the Vietnam War.

Kennedy graduated form Harvard College and the University of Virginia School of Law after serving in the US Naval Reserve. Prior to entering public office, he worked as a correspondent to the *Boston Post* and as an attorney in Washington D.C.. He rose to national acclaim as the chief counsel of the Senate Labor Rackets Committee from 1957 to 1959, when he publicly challenge Teamster's President Jimmy Hoffa over the corrupt practices of the union, and published *The Enemy Within,* a book about corruption in organized labor.

In March 1968 Kennedy began a campaign for the presidency and was a front-running candidate of the Democratic Party, appealing especially to black, Hispanic and Catholic voters. Kennedy was shot by Sirhan Sirhan, a Palestinian Arab.

Kennedy owned a home at the well-known Kennedy Compound on Cape Cod in Hyannis Port, but spent most of his time at his estate in McLean, Virginia, known as Hickory Hill, located west of Washington, D.C. His widow Ethel and their children continued to live at Hickory Hill after his death. She now lives full-time at the Hyannis Port home.[45]

THE ATTORNEY GENERAL
WASHINGTON

July 26, 1963

Dr. M. J. Bagley
61 East Frontier Boulevard
Henderson, Nevada

Dear Dr. Bagley:

My belated thanks for your letter requesting a pair of eyeglasses I have used for the collection. At long last, we have located a pair which are no longer useful. These are being mailed to you under separate cover.

Sincerely,

Attorney General

KIM HUNTER

Birth name:	Janet Cole
Born:	November 12, 1922
	Detroit Michigan, US
Died:	September 11, 2002 (aged 79)
	New York City, New York, US
Occupation:	Actress
Years Active:	1943-2002

> Kim was one of the few people whose letter
> sent to me handwritten, because in the world
> today practically all communication is done by
> email, text and mail.

Kim Hunter was born Janet Cole and was an American
film, theatre and television actress. She won both an
Academy Award and a Golden Globe Award, each as
Best Supporting Actress, for her performance as Stella
Kowalski in the 1951 film *A Streetcar Named Desire*.
Decades later she received a Daytime Emmy Award for
her work on the long-running soap *The Edge of Night*.

She was married to William Baldwin from 1944 to
1946 and Robert Emmett from 1951 to 2000.

Hunter died of a heart attack in New York City at
the age of 79. She received two stars on the Hollywood
walk of fame, one for her Motion Pictures at 1615 Vine
Street and a second for television at 1715 Vine Street.[46]

Kim Hunter

42 Commerce Street New York 14, New York

13 January, 1964

Dr. M. J. Bagley, Director
Famous People's Eye Glasses Museum
61 East Frontier Blvd.
Henderson, Nevada

Dear Dr. Bagley:

   The enclosed glasses are
truly mine — dilapidated,
out-of-date, and long in coming
to you — but mine — May they
find a cozy niche in your
museum —

    Best wishes,

     Sincerely,

      Kim Hunter

PRINCESS MARGARET, COUNTESS OF SNOWDON

Full Name:	Margaret Rose
House:	House of Windsor
Father:	George VI
Mother:	Elizabeth Bowes-Lyon
Born:	21 August 1930
	Glamis Castle, Scotland, UK
Died:	9 February 2002 (aged 71)
	King Edward VII Hospital, London, UK
Burial:	King George VI Memorial Chapel, St George's Chapel, Windsor Castle

Princess Margaret, Countess of Snowdon, was the only sibling of Queen Elizabeth II and the younger daughter of King George VI and Queen Elizabeth the Queen's mother.

Margaret spent much of her childhood years in the company of her older sister and parents. Her life changed dramatically in 1936, when her paternal uncle, King Edward VIII, abdicated to marry the divorced American Wallis Simpson. Margaret's father became King in Edward's place, and her older sister became heiress presumptive with Margaret second in line to the throne. During World War II, the two sisters stayed at Windsor Castle, despite government pressure to evacuate to Canada. During the war years, Margaret was not expected to perform any public or official duties, and instead continued her education.

After the war, Margaret fell in love with a recently divorced commoner 16 years her elder, Group Captain Peter Townsend, her father's equerry. Her father died in 1952, and her sister became queen. Margaret told her sister in early 1953 that she wished to marry Townsend. Many in the government felt that Townsend would be an unsuitable husband for the Queen's 22-year-old sister, and the Church of England refused to countenance the marriage to a divorced man. Her sister's coronation was pending, and Elizabeth asked Margaret to wait a year. Margaret eventually abandoned her plans, and, in 1960, accepted the proposal of the photographer Antony Armstrong-Jones, who was created Earl of Snowdon by Elizabeth II. The marriage, despite an auspicious start, soon became unhappy. The couple divorced in 1978, and Margaret never remarried.[47]

Whitehall 3141

KENSINGTON PALACE
W. 8

3rd April, 1964.

Dear Dr. Bagley,

I am bidden by Princess Margaret to write and
thank you for your letter.

As Her Royal Highness does not wear eye
glasses, I am afraid it is not possible for The Princess
to accede to your request.

Yours sincerely,

Jane Allday.

Lady-in-Waiting

Dr. M.J. Bagley,
Famous People's Eye Glasses Museum.

145

JAYNE MANSFIELD

Birth name:	Vera Jayne Palmer
Born:	April 19, 1933
	Bryn Mawr, Pennsylvania
Died:	June 29, 1967 (aged 34)
	Slidell, Louisiana
Cause of Death:	Traffic Accident
Other names:	Vera Jayne Peers, Vera Palmer
Education:	Southern Methodist University of Texas at Austin, University of California, Los Angeles.
Occupation:	Actress, singer, *Playboy* playmate, nightclub entertainer, model
Years Active:	1954-1967
Notable works:	*The Girl Can't Help it* (1956), *Will Success Spoil Rock Hunter?* (1957), *Too Hot to Handle* (1960), *The Waynard Bus* (1957) *Promises! Promises!* (1963)
Influenced by:	Marilyn Monroe
Influenced:	Anna Nicole Smith
Television:	*Follow the Sun* (1962), *Burk's Law* (1964), *What's My Line?* (1956-1966), *The Jack Benny Program* (1963), *The Bob Hope Show* (1957-1963), *The Ed Sullivan Show* (1957)
Spouse(s):	Paul Mansfield, Miklos Hargitay Jr., Matt Cimber

Children:	Jayne Marie Mansfield, Miklos "Mickey" Hargitay, Jr
	Zoltan Hargitay, Mariska Hargitay , Antonio "Tony" Cimber
Parents:	Herbert William Palmer and Vera Jeffrey Palmer Peers.
Awards:	Theatre World Award for *Promising Personality* (1956) Golden Globe for *New Star of The Year* – Actress (1957)

Jayne Mansfield is one of the several actresses who made it big in the Hollywood because of her well shaped body.

Jayne Mansfield was born Vera Jayne. She was an American actress in film, theatre, and television, a nightclub entertainer, a singer, and one of the early Playboy Playmates. She was a major Hollywood sex symbol of the 1950s and early 1960s. Mansfield was 20th Century Fox's alternative to Marilyn Monroe and came to be known as the Working Man's Monroe. She was also known for her well-publicized personal life and publicity stunts.

In the sexploitation film *Promises! Promises!* in 1963, she became the first major American actress to have a nude starring role in a Hollywood motion picture.

In 1967 Mansfield died in a car accident at the age of 34.[48]

Melvin J. Bagley

April 20, 1964

Dr. M. J. Bagley, Director
Famous People's Eye Glasses Museum
61 East Frontier Blvd.
Henderson, Nevada

Dear Dr. Bagley:

Thank you so much for your letter of March 19th
and the invitation to send a pair of my eye-glasses
for the museum. It is quite an honor.

I do not have any prescription glasses to send,
but have enclosed a very unique pair of green
sunshades which I hope will suffice.

Warmest Wishes,

JAYNE MANSFIELD

148

BARRY GOLDWATER

United States Senator from Arizona

January 3, 1969-January 3 1987

Birth name:	Barry Morris Goldwater
Born:	January 2, 1909
	Phoenix, Arizona Territory, US
Died:	May 29, 1998 (aged 89)
	Paradise Valley, Arizona, US
Resting Place:	Christ Church of the Ascension, Paradise Valley, Arizona
Political Party:	Republican
Spouse(s):	Margaret Johnson, Susan Shaffer Wechsler
Children:	Joanne, Barry Goldwater Jr., Michael and Margaret (Peggy)
Alma mater:	University of Arizona
Profession:	Businessman, politician
Religion:	Episcopalian
Service/branch:	United States Army Air Forces, Arizona Air National Guard, United States Air Force Reserve.
Years of Service:	1941-1945 (USAAF), 1945-1952 (ANG), 1952-1967 (USAFR)
Rank:	Lieutenant Colonel (USAAF, Colonel), Major general (USAFR)
Battles/War:	World War II, Korean War

> Barry Goldwater, 40 years ago, was a true hero
> to most conservative people in the United
> States.

Barry Morris Goldwater was a businessman and five-term United States Senator from Arizona, and the Republican Party's nominee for President in the 1964 election. He was known as "Mr. Conservative." An articulate and charismatic figure during the first half of the 1960s, Goldwater was the politician most often credited for sparking the resurgence of the American conservative political movement in the 1960s and libertarian movement.

Goldwater successfully urged President Richard Nixon to resign when evidence of a cover-up in the Watergate scandal became overwhelming and impeachment was imminent. By the 1980s, Goldwater became a vocal opponent of the religious right on issues such as abortion, gay rights, and the role of religion in public life.

He married Margaret "Peggy" Johnson. They had four children; Joanne, Barry, Michael, and Peggy. Barry became a widower in 1985. In 1992 he married Susan Wechsler, a nurse, 32 years his junior.[49]

BARRY GOLDWATER
ARIZONA

COMMITTEES:
ARMED SERVICES
LABOR AND PUBLIC WELFARE
SPECIAL COMMITTEE ON AGING

United States Senate
WASHINGTON, D.C.

June 3, 1964

Dr. N. J. Bagley, Director
Famous People's Eye Glasses Museum
61 East Frontier Boulevard
Henderson, Nevada

Dear Dr. Bagley:

I am flattered that you would wish to place a
pair of my eye glasses in the Famous People's
Eye Glasses Museum. So, under separate cover
one of my older pairs is being forwarded to
you for this purpose.

Sincerely,

Barry Goldwater
Barry Goldwater

LEON JAWORSKI

Born:	September 19, 1905
	Waco, McLennan County, Texas, U S A
Died:	December 9, 1982 (age 77)
	Wimberley, Hays County, Texas
Residence:	Houston, Texas
Alma mater:	Baylor Law School
	The George Washington University
Occupation:	Attorney, founder of Fulbright and Jaworski, Special prosecutor in Watergate scandal adjunct law professor
Political party:	Democratic, but frequently supported Republicans
Parents:	Marie Mira and Joseph Jaworski

Leonidas "Leon" Jaworski was the second special prosecutor during the Watergate Scandal. He was appointed to that position on November 1, 1973, soon after the Saturday Night Massacre of October 19–20, 1973, that resulted in the dismissal of his predecessor, Archibald Cox.

In 1925, he became the youngest person ever admitted to the Texas bar. After starting out defending bootleggers during Prohibition, in 1931 he joined the Houston law firm that became Fulbright and Jaworski, one of the largest law firms in the United States.[50]

LEON JAWORSKI

Bank of the Southwest Bldg.
HOUSTON, Texas 77002

These glasses were worn
by me while Watergate
Special Prosecutor —

Leon Jaworski

EDWARD G. ROBINSON

Birth name:	Emanuel Goldenberg
Born:	December 12, 1893
	Bucharest, Romania
Died:	January 26, 1973 (age 79)
	Los Angeles, California, U S
Occupation:	Actor
Years active:	1913–1973
Spouses:	Gladys Lloyd, Jane Robinson

Many great movies have starred Edward G. Robinson. I was delighted to receive this letter from him even though he did not send me any glasses.

Emanuel Goldenberg was a Romanian-born American actor. A popular star during Hollywood's Golden Age, he is best remembered for his roles as gangsters, such as Rico in his star-making film "Little Caesar" and as Rocco in "Key Largo", and performance as Sol Roth in "Soylent Green." Robinson was selected for an Honorary Academy Award for his work in the film industry, which was posthumously awarded two months after the actor's death in 1973. He was included in the American Film Institute's list of the 25 greatest male stars in American cinema. Other memorable roles include Barton

Keyes in the film "Indemnity", and Dathan in "The Ten Commandments".

Robinson spoke seven languages. He was never nominated for an Academy award, but in 1973 he was awarded an honorary Oscar in recognition that he had "achieved greatness as a player, a patron of the arts, and a dedicated citizen...in sum, a Renaissance man." He had been notified of the honor, but died two months before the award ceremony.

Robinson died of bladder cancer in 1973, and was buried in a crypt in the family mausoleum at Beth-El Cemetery in the Ridgewood area of the borough of Queens in New York City.[51]

Melvin J. Bagley

June 7
1 9 6 5

Dr. M. J. Bagley, Director
Famous People's Eye Glasses Museum
61 East Frontier Boulevard
Henderson, Nevada

Dear Dr. Bagley:

Yours is a museum most unique!

While I am flattered to be asked to contribute, I'm sure you will appreciate the
reason for my inability to do so. Like
most people who wear glasses, I am absent
minded as to where I last set them. As a
result, I keep many pairs strewn about the
house so that when I misplace one, there's
always another at hand.

By a strange coincidence, just today, I
visited my oculist and he tells me my eye-
sight hasn't changed a bit over the years.
Consequently, all my glasses are useful and
I wouldn't dare rid myself of any of them --
for the present, at least.

Cordially,

Edward G. Robinson

EGR:hh

RED SKELTON

Birth name:	Richard Bernard Skelton
Born:	July 18, 1913
	Vincennes, Indiana, U.S.
Died:	September 17, 1997 (aged 84)
	Rancho Mirage, California, U.S.
Medium:	Radio, Television, Film, Live performances
Years active:	1937-1981
Spouse:	Edna Marie Stilwell, Georgia Davis, and Lothian Toland
Emmy Awards:	1962 Best Comedy Program,
	1961 Outstanding Writing-Comedy Series,
	1986 Governors' Award

One time my wife and I went to see the Red Skelton show in Las Vegas. When he first came out and did his famous tumble, the audience literally roared with laughter. His true fans thought he was the funniest guy in the world.

Richard Bernard "Red" Skelton was an American entertainer best known for being a national radio and television comedian between 1937 and 1971. Skelton, who has stars on the Hollywood Walk of Fame, began his show business career in his teens as a circus clown and continued on vaudeville and Broadway and in films, radio, TV, nightclubs, and casinos, all while he pursued an entirely separate career as an artist.

He started working as a newspaper boy at the age of seven due to his father passing to help the family. In 1923, a man came up to the young Red and purchased all the newspapers he had and invited him to watch a show and gave him the ticket. The comedian, Ed Wynn, was part of the show and later took the young Skelton backstage. Skelton learned when he was young that he could make people laugh.

Skelton received a Lifetime Achievement Award from the Screen Actors guild in 1987; he was also one of the International Clown Hall of Fame's first inductees in 1989. He received several Emmy Awards.[52]

RICHARD RED SKELTON

June 14, 1965

Dr. M. J. Bagley
Famous People's Eye Glasses Museum
61 East Frontier Blvd.
Henderson, Nevada

Dear Dr. Bagley:

Mr. Skelton has asked me to respond to your
letter of May 26 inquiring whether he would
send you a pair of his old glasses.

Mr. Skelton does not care to do so.

Sincerely,

Mary Okie
Mary Okie
Secretary

ROBERT FROST

Birth name:	Robert Lee Frost
Born:	March 26, 1874
	San Francisco, California, United States
Died:	January 29, 1963 (age 88)
	Boston, Massachusetts, United States
Occupation:	Poet, playwright
Notable works:	*A Boy's Will, North of Boston*

> The only thing I know about Robert Frost is when I was in grade school we read some poetry he had written.

Robert Lee Frost was an American poet. He is highly regarded for his realistic depictions of rural life and his command of American colloquial speech. His work employed settings from rural life in New England in the early twentieth century, using them to examine complex social and philosophical themes. One of the most popular and critically respected American poets of his generation, Frost was honored frequently during his lifetime, receiving four Pulitzer Prizes for Poetry.

Robert Frost's personal life was plagued with grief and loss.

Elinor and Robert Frost had six children: son Elliot (1896–1904, died of cholera); daughter Lesley

Frost Ballantine (1899–1983), son Carol (1902–1940, committed suicide), daughter Irma (1903–1967), daughter Marjorie (1905–1934, died as a result of puerperal fever after childbirth), and daughter Elinor Bettina (died just three days after her birth in 1907). Only Leslie and Irma outlived their father. Frost's wife, who had heart problems throughout her life, developed breast cancer in 1937, and died of heart failure in 1938.[53]

"I'd like to get away from earth awhile
And then come back to it and begin over.
May no fate willfully misunderstand me
And half grant what I wish and snatch me away
Not to return. Earth's the right place for love:
I don't know where it's likely to go better.
I'd like to go by climbing a birch tree,
And climb black branches up a snow-white trunk
Toward heaven, till the tree could bear no more,
But dipped its top and set me down again.
That would be good both going and coming back.
One could do worse that be swinger of birches."
from "Birches"

STEVE ALLEN

Birth name:	Stephen Valentine Patrick
Born:	William Allen
	December 26, 1921
	New York, City
Died:	October 30, 2000 (aged 78)
	Los Angeles, California
Cause of death:	Heart attack, accident
Residence:	Los Angeles, California
Alma mater:	Arizona State Teachers College
Occupation:	Comedian, television personality, musician, writer
Years Active:	1940s-2000
Home town:	Chicago, Illinois
Spouse(s):	Dorothy Goodman (m. 1943-1952, divorced)
	Jane Meadows (m.1954-2000 his death)
Children:	Steve Jr., Brian, David and Bill

One time I received a letter from Steve Allen which instructed me on how to play a certain type of music. It was only then that I found out he had presided before some great late night show hosts like Johnny Carson.

Stephen Valentine Patrick William "Steve" Allen was an American television personality, musician, composer, actor, comedian, and writer. The first host of The Tonight Show, he hosted numerous game and variety shows, including *The Steve Allen Show*, *I've Got a Secret*, *The New Steve Allen Show* and was a regular panel member on CBS's *What's My Line?*

Allen was a credible pianist and a prolific composer, having penned over 14,000 songs one of which was recorded by Perry Como and others. Allen won a Grammy award in 1963 for best jazz composition, with his song "The Gravy Waltz". His vast number of songs have never been equaled. Allen wrote more than 50 books.

Allen made a last appearance on *The Tonight Show* on September 27, 1994, for the show's 40th anniversary broadcast. Jay Leno was effusive in praise and actually knelt down and kissed his ring.

On October 30, 2000, Allen was driving to his son's home in Encino, California, when his car was struck by another vehicle backing out of a driveway. Neither Allen nor the other driver believed he was injured and damage to both vehicles was minimal, so the two exchanged insurance information. Allen did not feel right and decided to take a nap. While napping, he suffered a massive heart attack and was pronounced dead shortly after 8 p.m. Autopsy results concluded that the traffic accident earlier in the day had caused a blood vessel in his chest to rupture, causing blood to leak into the sac surrounding the heart. In addition, he suffered four broken ribs as a result of the accident.

Allen has two stars on the Hollywood Walk of Fame—a television star at 1720 Vine St. and a radio star at 1537 Vine St.[54]

STEVE ALLEN
15720 VENTURA BOULEVARD
ENCINO, CALIFORNIA
SUITE 503

February
Eleventh
1 9 6 6

Dr. M. J. Bagley, Director
Famous People's Eye Glasses Museum
61 East Frontier Boulevard
Henderson, Nevada

Dear Dr. Bagley:

Please forgive the delay in getting the enclosed
glasses to you, but it took some time to locate
an additional pair for your collection.

My Optometrist, Dr. Irving W. Alpert of Sherman
Oaks was kind enough to locate a pair of glasses
that I have worn for many years. They were dis-
carded when I changed my prescription and started
wearing black frames. They were, however, made
especially for me and you will note that they have
a special coating so that there is no light reflection
which was indeed a problem under TV lights.

I trust that they will serve your purpose and I am
happy to donate them to your Museum.

Cordially,

Steve Allen

SA/d
Enclosure: (1)

HENRY CABOT LODGE, JR.

Lieutenant Colonel United Stare
Army World War II

Born:	July 5, 1002
	Nahant, Massachusetts
Died:	February 27, 1985 aged 82
	Beverly, Massachusetts
Nationality:	American
Political Party:	Republican
Spouse:	Emily Esther Sears
Children:	George Cabot Lodge II, Henry Sears Lodge
Alma Mater:	Harvard University
Religion:	Episcopalian

> The name Henry Cabot Lodge II always intrigued me greatly because it seems like an unusual name. I was more than elated when he sent me a letter that he himself had signed.

Henry Cabot Lodge, Jr. was a Republican, United States Senator of Massachusetts. He was the third United States Ambassador to the United Nations under President Dwight D. Eisenhower, United States Ambassador to South Vietnam under President John F. Kennedy and Lyndon B. Johnson, and United States Ambassador to West Germany under President Lyndon B. Johnson. He was the Republican nominee for Vice President in the 1960 Presidential election.

His father was George Cabot Lodge, a poet, through whom he was a grandson of Senator Henry Cabot Lodge and great great great grandson of Senator George Cabot. In 1926, Lodge married Emily Esther Sears. They had two children George Cabot Lodge II (b. 1927) and Henry Sears Lodge (b. 1930). In 1966 he was elected an honorary member of the Massachusetts Society of the Cincinnati.

Lodge died in 1985 and was interred in the Mount Auburn Cemetery in Cambridge, Massachusetts.[55]

Henry Cabot Lodge

Beverly, Massachusetts
June 8, 1965

Dr. M. J. Bagley
Director
Famous People's Eye Glasses Museum
61 East Frontier Boulevard
Henderson, Nevada

Dear Doctor Bagley:

In reply to your recent letter, I am sorry to say I have no extra pair of eye glasses.

Sincerely yours,

Henry Cabot Lodge

KYLE ROTE

Date of birth:	October 27, 1928
Place of birth:	San Antonio, Texas
Date of death:	August 15, 2002 (aged 73)
Place of death:	Baltimore Maryland
Position(s):	Halfback, Wide receiver
College:	Southern Methodist
NFL Draft:	1951/Round 1/Pick: 1
1951-1961:	New York Giants
Career Highlights and Awards:	Pro Bowls 4

Ever since I received this letter from Mr. Rote, I have been a loyal fan of the New York Giants. It would be interesting to know what happened to his son that threw the pass that broke his glasses. This letter that he wrote is truly unique.

William Kyle Rote, Sr. was an All-American running back at Southern Methodist University, class of 1951, played for 11 years for the New York Giants, 1951–1961. Following his playing career, Rote served as the Giants backfield coach and was sports broadcaster for WNEW radio, NBC, and WNBC New York.

Rote was the son Jack and Emma Belle Owens Rote. His family suffered tragedies during World War

II, and when he was 16 years old his mother was killed in a car accident and his older brother Jack was killed on Iwo Jima.

After graduating from high school in 1947, Rote accepted an athletic scholarship to Southern Methodist University where he became one of the most celebrated collegiate football players in the country. He was voted by the Texas Sportswriters Association as "The Outstanding Individual Performance by a Texas Athlete in the First Half of the 20th century."

The New York Giants selected Rote with first pick in the 1951 NFL Draft. He started out as a running back, but after the first two years switched to wide receiver due to a knee injury. When Rote retired after his 1961 season, he had become the Giant's career leader in pass receptions (300), receiving yardage (4,805), and touchdown receptions (48). He was second highest in total touchdowns (56) and fifth-leading scorer (312) points. His average gain per catch was 15.9 yards.

Rote and his first wife, Betty Jamison, had four children—Kyle, Gary, Chris and Elizabeth. His oldest son Kyle Rote, Jr. was one of the first notable soccer stars from the United States.

Rote authored the books, *Pro Football for the Fans* and *The language of Pro Football,* and wrote the *Giants Fight Song.* He also published two volumes of poetry, was an ASCAP songwriter, accomplished pianist, and oil painter having a number of his works shown at museums throughout the United States.[56]

WNEW Radio

565 FIFTH AVENUE, NEW YORK, NEW YORK 10017, YUKON 6-7000   METROPOLITAN BROADCASTING RADIO

July 8, 1966

Dr. M. J. Bagley, Director
Famous People's Eye Glasses Museum
61 East Frontier Boulevard
Henderson, Nevada

Dear Dr. Bagley:

Thank you for your very flattering request. Please do not
assume from the condition of my glasses that I actually
wore them in a game! These were broken by an extremely
accurate "bullet pass" from the arm of my 16 year old son.

Kindest regards,

Kyle Rote

KR:eb   Kyle Rote
Encl.   Sports Director

VANESSA REDGRAVE

Born:	30 January 1937
	Greenwich, London, England UK
Occupation:	Actress
Years active:	1958-present
Spouse(s)	Tony Richardson (in. 1962-1967, divorced)
	Franco Nero (in. 2006-present)
Children:	Natasha Richardson (deceased), Joely Richardson, Carlo Gabriel Nero

> The glasses I received from Vanessa Redgrave are probably the least worn of any of the glasses in the museum. What a sweetheart she is to send me a brand new pair.

Vanessa Redgrave is an English actress of stage, screen and television, as well as a political activist.

Redgrave was born in Greenwich, London, the daughter of actors Sir Michael Redgrave and Rachel Kempton.

Redgrave was married to Director Tony Richardson in 1962. Together they had two children Natasha Richardson and Joely Richardson. They divorced in 1967, Tony left her for the French actress Jeanne. She became romantically involved with Italian Actor Franco Nero, together they had a son Carlo Gabriel Redgrave

Sparanero, known professionally as Carlo Gabriel Nero, a screenwriter and director. After separating for many years, during which they both had relationships with other people, they reunited and married on December 31, 2006. Carlo Nero directed Redgrave in the cinematic adaptation of Wallace Shawn's play *The Fever*.

Redgrave rose to prominence in 1961 playing Rosalind in "As You Like It" with the Royal Shakespeare Company and has since made more than 35 appearances on London's West End and Broadway, winning both the Tony and Olivier Awards. On screen, she has starred in more than 80 films; including *Blowup* in 1966, *Isadora* in 1968, *Mary Queen of Scots* in 1971, *The Devils* in 1971, *Julia* in 1977, *The Bostonians* in 1984, *Howards End* in 1992, *Mission: Impossible* in 1996 and *Atonement* in 2007. Redgrave was proclaimed by Arthur Miller and Tennessee Williams as "the greatest living actress of our times," and she remains the only British actress ever to win the Oscar, Emmy, Tony, Cannes, Golden Globe, and the Screen Actors Guild awards. She was also the recipient of the 2010 BAFTA Fellowship "in recognition of an outstanding and exceptional contribution to film."[57]

Dear Dr Bagley— These are a pair of glasses I had made for myself November 1966 but have only worn them about 10 minutes for reasons that will be immediately obvious to you! I threw away my really used old specs just before your letter came — anyway perhaps these will do & they come with my best wishes. Yrs sincerely Vanessa Redgrave

JULIE CHRISTIE

Birth name:	Julie Frances Christie
Born:	14 April 1941
	Chabua, Assam, British India
Occupation:	Actress, activist
Years active:	1957-present
Spouse(s):	Duncan Campbell (2007- present)

I am surprised to find so many talented people in the world that don't wear prescription glasses. This is another case were she is kind enough to send her sunglasses.

Julie Frances Christie is a British Actress. A pop icon of the swinging London" era of the 1960s, she has won the Academy. Golden Globe, BAFTA, and Screen Actors Guild Awards.

Christie's first big-screen roles were in *Crooks Anonymous* and *The Fast Lady* both in 1962, and her break through was in 1963s, *Billy Liar*, in 1965, she won an Academy Award for Best Actress for her performance as Diana Scott in *Darling*. That same year, she starred as Lara Antipova in *Doctor Zhivago*, the eighth highest grossing film of all time after adjustment for inflation. In the following years, she starred in *Fahrenheit 451* in 1966, *Far From the Madding Crowd* in 1967, *Petulia* in 1968,

McCabe & Mrs. Miller in 1971, *Don't Look Now* in 1973, and *Heaven Can Wait* in 1978.

Christie's acting work became low-key in the 1980s.

She is active in various causes, including animal rights, environmental protection, and the anti-nuclear power movement and is also a Patron of the Palestine Solidarity Campaign, as well as Reprieve.[58]

```
                                  Yellow Ferry Harbor
                                  Sausalito, California


                                  July 28, 1967


Dr. M. J. Bagley
Director
Famous People's Eye Glasses Museum
61 East Frontier Boulevard
Henderson, Nevada


Dear Dr. Bagley,

        I would be very pleased to send you
a pair of eye glasses for the Famous People's
Eye Glasses Museum, only I have never worn
glasses, would sun glasses do?

            With best wishes,

                                              have her
                                              glasses


                Julie Christie




JC/sdgh
```

ED BEGLEY

Birth name:	Edward James Begley
Born:	March 25, 1901
	Hartford, Connecticut, US
Died:	April 28, 1970 (aged 69)
	Hollywood, California, US
Cause of Death:	Heart attack
Occupation:	Film, television, radio actor
Years active:	1917-1970
Spouse(s):	Amanda Huff, Dorothy Reeves, Helen Jordan

> I was always fascinated with the name Ed
> Begley for it is so close to my own name. The
> Bagley name was the result of several changes
> and who knows it might have been Begley.

Edward James "Ed" Begley. Sr. was an Academy
Award-winning American actor of theatre, radio, film,
and television.

Begley was born in Hartford, Connecticut, the son
of Hannah Clifford and Michael Joseph Begley, Irish
immigrants. Begley began his career as a Broadway and
radio actor while in his teens. He appeared in the hit
musical "Going Up" on Broadway in 1917 and in London
the next year. He later acted in roles as Sgt. O'Hara in
the radio show "The Fat Man." His radio work included

a period as Charlie Chan and Stroke of Fate amongst other roles. He also starred in the 1950s radio program *Richard Diamond, Private Detective,* playing Lieutenant Walter Levinson, head of homicide at the 5th Precinct, Manhattan. In the late 1940s, he began appearing regularly in supporting film roles. He was elected a member of The Lambs in 1943.

He won the Academy Award for Best Supporting Actor for his role in *Sweet Bird of Youth* in 1962.

His other television work included appearances on *Justice, Empire, The Virginian, Bonanza, The Fugitive, Target: The Corruptors,* and *Going My Way,* with Gene Kelly.

Begley married three times. Amanda Huff from 1922 to 1957, Dorothy Reeves from 1961 to 1963, Helen Jordan from 1963–1970. He is the father of the actor and environmental advocate Ed Begley, Jr.

Among his many Broadway credits were *All My Sons* and *Inherit the Wind.*

Begley died of a heart attack in Hollywood, California. He is buried at the San Fernando Mission Cemetery in Mission Hills.[59]

ED BEGLEY

June 29, 1969
P.O. Box 495
Northridge Calif.
91324

Dr. M. J. Bagley
Director
Famous People's Eye Glasses Museum
61 East Lake Mead Drive
Henderson Nevada

Dear Dr. Bagley:

Enclosed is a pair of my eye glasses to be added to your museum collection as per your written request.

Yours sincerely
Ed Begley

KAYE BALLARD

Birth name:	Catherine Gloria Balotta
Born:	November 20, 1925
	Cleveland, Ohio US
Occupation:	Actress, singer
Years Active:	1951-present

> I thought it was quite cute when she wrote in her letter, "How Dare you know I need glasses!" This phrase was typical of Kaye Ballard's humor. I also considered using this phrase as the title of the book.

Kaye Ballard is an American musical theatre and television actress, comedienne, and singer. Ballard was born Catherine Gloria Balatta in Cleveland, Ohio, one of four children born to Italian emigrant parents, Lena Nacarato and Vincenzo Balotta. She has three siblings: Orlando, Jean and Rosalie. Kay established herself as a musical comedienne in the 1940s, joining the Spike Jones touring revue of entertainers. She is capable of playing broad physical comedy as well as stand-up dialogue routines, she became familiar in television and stage productions. A phrase her mother had used when Kaye was a child, "Good luck with your MOUTH!" became her catchphrase in her sketches and on television. During

1954, she was the first person to record the song "In Other Words" later renamed "Fly Me to the Moon."

In 1957, she and Alice Ghostley played the two wicked stepsisters in the live telecast of Rogers and Hammerstein's *Cinderella,* starring Julie Andrews in the title role. In 1962, she released an LP, *Peanuts* on which she played Lucy van Pelt from the comic strip namesake of the album with Arthur Siegel playing Charlie Brown. From 1967–69, she co-starred as Kaye Buell, a woman whose son marries her next door neighbors daughter, in the NBC sitcom "The Mothers-in-Law," with Eve Arden playing her neighbor. She also appeared as regular on "The Doris Day Show" as restaurant owner Angie Pallucci from 1970–72. She made appearances on the American Television game show *Match Game.* In 1976, she was a guest star on *The Muppet Show.* She also appeared on the TV series *Alice,* in which she played a kleptomaniac phony medium, as well as *Daddy Dearest* where she guest-starred opposite Don Rickles as a DMV clerk.

Ballard starred on Broadway as Helen in "The Golden Apple," introducing the song "Lazy Afternoon." She portrayed Rosalie in "Carnival" with Jerry Orbach, Ruth in Joseph Papp's production of "The Pirates of Penzance" and the title role in "Molly." She created the role of the Countess and closed out-of-town in Marc Blitzstein's "Reuben, Reuben" and played Ruth Sherwood in *Wonderful Town at New York Center* in 1963.

In 1995, a Golden Palm Star on the Palm Springs, California, Walk of Stars was dedicated to her.

A breast cancer survivor, Ballard has never married. She currently lives in Rancho Mirage, California. The house she lived in was once owned by her friend, Desi Arnaz, and she bought it from him, after staying there while she worked on *The Mothers-in-Law*.[60]

Kay Ballard
July 25, 1971

Dear Dr. Bagley:

Here are the glasses you requested. They are mine. And how dare you know that I need glasses anyway!

Peace!

Kay Ballard

ANNE BAXTER

Born:	May 7, 1923
	Michigan City, Indiana, US
Died:	December 12, 1985 (aged 62)
	New York City, New York, US
Cause of Death:	Brain aneurysm
Occupation:	Actress
Years Active:	1940-85
Spouse(s):	John Hodiak, Randolph Gait, David Klee
Children:	Katrina Hodiak, Melissa Gait, Maginel Gait
Parents:	Kenneth Stuart Baxter, Catherine Wright

In following the lives of many famous people most of those people became famous on their own. Not many many people are born into fame and expand the role.

Anne Baxter was an American actress known for her performances in films such as *The Magnificent Ambersons* in 1942, *The Razor's Edge* in 1946, *All About Eve* in 1950 and *The Ten Commandments* in 1956.

Baxter was born in Michigan City, Indiana, to Kenneth Stuart Baxter and Catherine Wright, whose father was the famed architect Frank Lloyd Wright. Kenneth Baxter was a prominent executive with the Seagram's Distillery Co. and was raised in New York

City. At age 10, Baxter attended a Broadway play starring Helen Hayes, and was so impressed that she declared to her family that she wanted to become an actress. By the age of 13, she had appeared on Broadway. During this period, Baxter learned her acting craft as a student of the famed teacher Maria Ouspenskaya.

Baxter is also remembered for her role as the Egyptian Queen Nefertari opposite Charlton Heston's portrayal of Moses in Cecil B. DeMile's award winning, "The Ten Commandments" (1956). She appeared regularly on television in the 1960s. She did a stint as one of the *"What's My Line?"* "Mystery Guests". She also starred as guest villain "Zelda the Great" in two episodes of the superhero show Batman. She appeared as another villain, "Olga, Queen of the Cossacks," Opposite Vincent Price's "Egghead" in three episodes of the show's third season. She also played an old flame of Raymond Burr on his crime series "Ironside."

Anne Baxter suffered a brain aneurysm on December 4, 1985, while hailing a taxi on Madison Avenue in New York City. She died 8 days later at Lenox Hill Hospital at 62.

Baxter has a star on the Hollywood Walk of Fame at 6741 Hollywood Blvd.[61]

Melvin J. Bagley

St-Regis - Sheraton
Fifth Avenue and Fifty-Fifth Street
New York, N. Y. 10022

July 30, 1971

Dr. M.J. Bagley, Director
Famous People's Eye Glasses Museum
61 East Lake Mead Drive
Henderson, Nevada   89015

Dear Mr. Bagley -

As of this date, I do not wear
eye glasses, for which I thank the Good Lord!

All good wishes.

Sincerely,

[signature]

Anne Baxter

AB:dlb

182

PHYLLIS DILLER

Born:	Phyllis Ada Driver
	July 17, 1917
	Lima, Ohio, US
Died:	August 20, 2012 (aged 95)
	Brentwood, Los Angeles California, US
Cause of death:	Natural causes
Alma mater	Bluffton College
Occupation:	Actress, Comedienne
Years Active:	1952-2012
Spouse(s):	Sherwood Anderson Diller, Warde Donovan (Tatum)
Partner(s)	Robert P. Hasting

In following the life of Phyllis Diller, the main thing that sticks in my mind was her wild hairdo.

Phyllis Diller was an American actress and comedienne. She created a stage persona of a wild-haired and eccentrically dressed housewife who made self-deprecating jokes about her age and appearance. Her terrible cooking, and a husband named Fang," was entirely fictional, while pretending to smoke from a long cigarette holder.

Diller, a longtime resident of Brentwood, credited much of her success to Bob Hope, in large part because he included her in many of his movies and his Vietnam USO shows. She was an accomplished pianist and a painter.

Diller credited much of her success to a motivational book, *The Magic of Believing* (1948) by Claude M. Bistol, which gave her confidence at the start of her career. The book was also an inspiration for her friend, Liberace.

Diller was married and divorced twice. She had six children from her marriage to her first husband, Sherwood Anderson Diller. Dillers' second husband was actor Warde Donovan (born Warde Tatum), whom she married on October 7, 1965 until she divorced Donovan in 1975. She was the partner of Robert P. Hastings from 1985 until his death on May 23, 1996.

She candidly discussed her plastic surgery, a series of procedures first undertaken when she was 55. In her 2006 autobiography, she wrote that she had undergone "fifteen different procedures". Her numerous surgeries were the subject of a 20/20 segment February 12, 1993.

Diller penned her autobiography in 2005, titled *Like a Lampshade in a Whorehouse*. Diller spent much of her final years painting, cooking, and gardening.

On the morning of August 20, 2012, Diller died from natural causes in her Brentwood, Los Angeles, California home at the age of 95 with a "smile on her face" according to her family.[62]

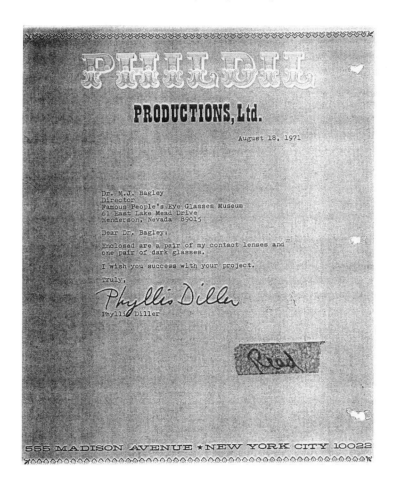

PHILDIL
PRODUCTIONS, Ltd.

August 18, 1971

Dr. M.J. Bagley
Director
Famous People's Eye Glasses Museum
61 East Lake Mead Drive
Henderson, Nevada 89015

Dear Dr. Bagley:

Enclosed are a pair of my contact lenses and
one pair of dark glasses.

I wish you success with your project.

Truly,

Phyllis Diller

Phyllis Diller

555 MADISON AVENUE ★ NEW YORK CITY 10022

ROBERT GOULET

Birth name:	Robert Gerard Goulet
Born:	November 26, 1933
	Lawrence, Massachusetts, US
Died:	October 30, 2007 (aged 73)
	Los Angeles, California, US
Education:	Victoria Composite High School
Alma mater:	The Royal Conservatory of Music
Occupation:	Singer, actor
Years Active:	1952-2007
Spouse(s)	Louise Longmore (1956-1963)
	Carol Lawrence (1963-1981)
	Vera Novak (1982-2007) his death

I was a loyal UNLV basketball fan in the late, as was Robert. Several times he was asked to sing the National anthem at the beginning of the game, which he gracefully accepted.

Robert Gerard Goulet was an American singer and actor. He originated the role of Lancelot in the 1960 Broadway musical *Camelot* and made numerous appearances in Las Vegas.

Goulet was born in Lawrence, Massachusetts, the only son of Jeanette Gauthier and Joseph Georges André Goulet, a laborer. His parents were both of

French Canadian ancestry. He was a descendant of French-Canadian pioneers Zacharie Cloutiert and Jacques Goulet. Shortly after his father's death, 13-year-old Robert moved with his mother and sister Claire to Girouxville, Alberta, and he spent his formative years in Canada.

Due to the Canadian citizenship law at the time, Goulet was not awarded Canadian citizenship despite his Canadian parents, making him a Lost Canadian. A 2008 law would have allowed him to retroactively be granted citizenship, but he died before it was received.

After living in Girouxville, Alberta, for several years, they moved to the provincial capital of Edmonton to take advantage of the performance opportunities offered in the city. There, he attended the famous voice schools founded by Herbert G. Turner and Jean Letourneau, and later became a radio announcer for radio station, CKUA. Upon graduating from Victoria Composite high school, Goulet received a scholarship to The Royal Conservatory of Music in Toronto. There, he studied voice with famed oratorio baritones, George Lambert and Ernesto Vinci.

He was married three times; Louise Longmore from 1956 to1963, had daughter Nicolette, Carol Lawrence from 1963 to 1981, had two sons Christopher and Michael, and Vera Novak from 1982 to 2007.

In 2006, he received a star on Canada's Walk of Fame.[63]

Robert Goulet

4th Sept. 1971

But Dr. Bagley, I don't
use eye glasses!

Will sun-glasses do?

Robert Goulet

Robert Goulet

ans Sept 13

RG:jd

188

Robert Goulet

5th October 1971

Dear Dr. Bagley,

You are fortunate!

This is the only pair of
sun glasses that in all
my life I have neither
broken nor lost!

Robert Goulet

RG:jd

PAUL ANKA

Birth name:	Paul Albert Anka
Born:	July 30, 1941
	Ottawa, Ontario
Genres:	Pop, jazz, soft rock, doo-wop
Occupations:	Singer, songwriter
Instruments:	Vocals, piano, guitar
Years active:	1955 – present
Labels:	EMI Columbia, RCA Columbia

> When Frank Sinatra sings, "My Way", it seems to me like a completely different type of song. When I found out that PaulAnka had written the great song, I could not help but put him in a class with Irving Berlin and Cole Porter.

Paul Albert Anka, is a Canadian-American singer, songwriter, and actor. Anka became famous in the late 1950s and 1960s with hit songs like "Diana," "Lonely Boy," and "Put Your Head on My Shoulder." He went on to write such well-known music as the theme for The Tonight Show Starring Johnny Carson and one of Tom Jones' biggest hits, "She's a Lady," and the English lyrics for Frank Sinatra's signature song, "My Way."

Paul Anka was born to Andy and Camelia Anka in Ottawa, Ontario, where they owned a restaurant called

The Locanda. His parents are both from Greek Orthodox Lebanese descent. He sang with the St. Elias Antiochian Orthodox Church choir under the direction of Frederick Karam, with whom he studied music theory. He studied piano with Winnifred Rees. Anka attended Fisher Park High School and Lisgar Collegiate Institute.

Anka became a naturalized US citizen in 1990.

Anka was married to Anne de Zogheb, the daughter of Lebanese diplomat Charles de Zogheb from February 16, 1963 until September 28, 2000. They met in 1962 in San Juan, Puerto Rico, where she was a fashion model on assignment, under contract to the Eileen Ford Agency. Zogheb, raised in Egypt, is of English, Lebanese, French Dutch, and Greek decent. The coupe married the following year in a ceremony at Paris-Orly Airport. She quit modeling after their second child was born. They have five daughters, Amelia, Anthea, Alicia, Amanda (who's married to actor Jason Bateman) and Alexandra.

In 2008, Anka married his personal Trainer, Anna Aberg, in Sardinia. They divorced in 2010 and share custody of their son, Ethan.

In 1972, a street in Ottawa was named Paul Anka Drive. In 1981, the Ottawa City Council named August 26th as "Paul Anka Day," to celebrate his quarter century in show business.

Anka has written an autobiography. *"My Way"* co-written with David Dalton with a forward by Paul Holmgren.[64]

PAUL ANKA PRODUCTIONS

TWO HUNDRED WEST FIFTY SEVENTH STREET • NEW YORK, N. Y. 10019 • (212) 582-5463

August 20, 1971

Dr. M. J. Bagley
Director
Famous People's Eye Glasses Museum
61 East Lake Mead Drive
Henderson, Nevada 89015

Dear Dr. Bagley:

      I would be most pleased to have
a pair of my eye glasses added to your
museum. Therefore, I will be sending
you a pair in the near future.

      Very truly yours,

Paul Anka

PA:jaj

ARTIE SHAW

Birth Name:	Arthur Jacob Arshawsky
Born:	May 23, 1910
	New York City, New York, US
Died:	December 30, 2004 (aged 94)
	Thousand Oaks, California, US
Genres:	Swing, big band
Occupations:	Bandleader, composer
Instruments:	Clarinet
Years active:	1925-2004

The letter that we received from Artie Shaw is one of a kind, in the respect that he requested a receipt for a contribution that is tax deductible.

Artie Shaw was born Arthur Jacob Arshawsky. He was an American clarinetist, composer, bandleader and author. Shaw wrote both fiction and non-fiction.

He was widely regarded as "one of jazz's finest clarinetists and led one of the United States' most popular big bands in the late 1930s through the early 1940s. Their signature song, a 1938 version of Cole Porters "Begin the Beguine" was a wildly successful single and one of the era's defining recordings. Shaw was also an early proponent of Third Stream, which blended classical and jazz and recorded some small-group sessions that flirted with be-bop before retiring from music in 1954.

A self-proclaimed "very difficult man," Shaw was married eight times: Jane Cairns from 1932 to 1933; this marriage was annulled, Margaret Allen from 1934 to 1937; this marriage ended in divorce, actress Lana Turner in 1940; this marriage ended in divorce, Betty Kern, the daughter of songwriter Jerome Kern from 1942–1943; this marriage ended in divorce, actress Ava Gardner from 1945 to 1946; this marriage ended in divorce, Kathleen Winsor from 1946 to 1948; this marriage was annulled, actress Doris Dowling from 1952 to 1956; this marriage ended in divorce, actress Evelyn Keyes from 1957 to 1985; this marriage ended in divorce. He has two sons, Steven Kern Shaw and Jonathan Dowling Shaw. Both Lana Turner and Ava Gardner later described Shaw as being extremely emotionally abusive. His controlling nature and incessant verbal abuse in fact drove Turner to have a nervous breakdown. Shaw even briefly dated actress Judy Garland in 1940.

Artie Shaw made several musical shorts in 1939 for Vitaphone and Paramount Pictures. He portrayed himself in the Fred Astaire film, *Second chorus* in 1940, which featured Shaw and his orchestra playing "Concerto for Clarinet." The film brought him two Oscar nominations, one for Best Score and one for Best Song "Love of My Life."[65]

ARTIE SHAW

Tower 58
58 West 58th Street
New York, New York 10019

September 8, 1971

Dr. M. J. Bagley, Director
Famous People's Eye Glasses Museum
61 East Lake Mead Drive
Henderson, Nevada 89015

Dear Dr. Bagley:

Thank you for your letter of August 27th. In
response to your request, enclosed you will
find an old, and definitely authentic pair of
Mr. Shaw's eye glasses for your museum.

Our accountant has informed me that this contribution is tax deductable. For our records
a receipt in the amount of $47.50 will be
greatly appreciated.

Thank you very much.

Cordially,

Claire Zock
Secretary to Mr. Shaw

/cmz
Enclosure

PETER SELLERS

Birth name:	Richard Henry Sellers
Born:	8 September 1925
	Southsea, Portsmouth
	England, UK
Died:	24 July 1980 (age 54)
	London, England, UK
Occupation:	Actor, comedian and singer
Years Active:	1948-1980
Known for:	Character actor and improvisation
Spouse(s):	Ann Howe, Britt Ekland, Miranda Quarry, Lynne Frederick

I was always intrigued with Peter Seller's ability to play. Damn, it is brilliant.

Peter Sellers, born Richard Henry Sellers, was a British film actor, comedian and singer. He appeared in the BBC Radio comedy series *The Goon Show*, featured on a number of hit comic songs and became known to a worldwide audience through his many film characterizations, among them Chief Inspector Clouseau in *The Pink Panther* series of films.

Sellers began as a film actor at 25. Although the bulk of his work was comedic-based, often parodying characters of authority such as military officers or policemen, he also performed in other film genres and roles. Sellers's versatility enabled him to portray a wide range of comic characters using different accents and guises, and he would often assume multiple roles within the same film, frequently with contrasting temperaments and styles. He was nominated three times for an Academy Award, twice for the Academy Award for Best Actor for his performances in *Dr. Strangelove* and *Being There*, and once for the Academy Award for Best Live Action Short Film for *The Running Jumping & Standing Still* Film (1960). He won the BAFTA Award for Best Actor in a Leading Role twice, for *I'm All Right Jack* and for the original Pink Panther film, *The Pink Panther* (1963) and was nominated as Best Actor three times. In 1980 he won the Golden Globe Award for Best Actor –Motion Picture Musical or Comedy for his role in *Being There,* and also earned three other Golden Globe nominations in the same category. Turner Classic Movies called Sellers, "one of the most accomplished comic actors of the late 20th century."

In his personal life, Sellers struggled with depression and insecurities. He had three children from his first two marriages. He died as a result of a heart attack in 1980, aged 54. Filmmakers the Boulting brothers described Sellers as "the greatest comic genius this country has produced since Charles Chaplin."[66]

PETER SELLERS

13 September, 1971

                              c/o Theo Cowan
                              45 Clarges Street
                              London W1

Famous People's Eye Glasses Museum
61 East Lake Mead Drive
Henderson, Nevada 89015

Attention: Dr. M.J. Bagley
            Director

Dear Dr. Bagley:

     I gives me great pleasure to send you the
enclosed eye glasses. I declare that I have
peered through them on numerous occasions.

                    Sincerely,

                    PETER SELLERS

PS:ml
Enclosure

LILLIAN GISH

Birth name:	Lillian Diana Gish
Born:	October 14, 1893
	Springfield, Ohio, United States
Died:	February 27, 1993 (age 99)
	New York City, New York, United States
Occupation:	Actress
Years:	1912–1987

Lillian Diana Gish born was an American stage, screen and television actress whose film acting career spanned 75 years, from 1912 to 1987. She was called "The First Lady of American Cinema."

She was a prominent film star of the 1910s and 1920s, particularly associated with the films of director D. W. Griffith, including her leading role in Griffith's seminal *Birth of a Nation* (1915). Her sound-era film appearances were sporadic, but included memorable roles in the controversial western *Duel in the Sun* (1946) and the offbeat thriller *Night of the Hunter* (1955). She did considerable television work from the early 1950s into the 1980s, and closed her career playing, for the first time, opposite Belle Davis in the 1987 film *The Whales of August*.

The American Film Institute (AFI) named Gish 17th among the greatest female stars of all time. She was awarded an Honorary Academy Award in 1971, and in 1984 she received an AFI Life Achievement Award.

Gish never married or had children. Gish maintained a very close relationship with her sister Dorothy, as well as with Mary Pickford, for her entire life. Another of her closest friends was Helen Hayes, Gish was the godmother of Hayes son James MacArthur.

Gish died in her sleep of natural cause at the age of 99, and is interred beside her sister Dorothy at St. Bartholomew's Episcopal Church in New York City. Her estate, which she left to Hayes who died a month later, was valued at several million dollars, and went to provide prizes for artistic excellence.[67]

Lillian Gish

September 23rd, 1971

Dear Dr. Bagley,

Fortunately, from Miss Gish's point of view, she has never worn eye glasses in her entire life.

Very truly yours,

James Frasher
Tour Manager
for
Miss Lillian Gish

JIMMY DURANTE

Birth name:	James Francis Durante
Born:	February 10, 1893
	Brooklyn, New York, US
Died:	March 29, 1980 (aged 87)
	Santa Monica, California, US
Other names:	The Schnoz, The Great Schnozzola
Occupation:	Actor, comedian, singer, pianist
Years active:	1920-1972
Spouse(s)	Jeanne Olson, Margie Little

> When I hear the name Jimmy Durante, it makes me think of the song "Inka Dinka Doo". I could not imagine anyone singing such a funny song, especially in such a horrible voice, and still become popular.

James Francis "Jimmy" Durante was an American singer, pianist, comedian, and actor. His distinctive clipped gravelly speech, comic language butchery, jazz influenced songs, and large nose helped make him one of America's most familiar and popular personalities of the 1920s through the 1970s. His jokes about his nose included referring to it as a Schnozzola, and the word became his nickname. Durante's radio show was bracketed with two trademarks: "Inka Dinka Doo" as his opening theme, and the invariable signoff that became another familiar national catchphrase: "Good night, Mrs. Calabash, wherever you are." For years Durante preferred to keep the mystery alive. Durante's first wife was the former Jean (Jeanne) Olson, whom he married on June 19, 1921. She died on Valentine's Day in 1943, after a lingering heart ailment of about two years. Durante married his second wife, Margaret "Margie" Little, at St. Malachy's Catholic Church in New York City on December 14, 1960. She was 41, he 67, when they married. With help from their attorney Mary G. Rogan, the couple was able to adopt a baby, Cecilia Alicia on Christmas Day, 1961. CeCe became a champion horsewoman and then a horse trainer and horseback-riding instructor near San Diego, married a computer designer Stephen, and has two sons and a daughter Connor, Ryan and Maddie. Margaret died on June 7, 2009, at age 90.

On August 15, 1958, for his charitable acts, Durante was awarded a huge three-foot-high brass loving cup by the Al Bahr Shriners Temple. The inscription read: "JIMMY DURANTE THE WORLD'S MOST FAMOUS COMEDIAN. A loving cup to you Jimmy, it's larger than your nose, but smaller than your heart. Happiness always, Al Bahr Temple, August 15, 1958."[68]

September 29, 1971

Dr. M. J. Bagley
Director
FAMOUS PEOPLE'S EYE GLASSES MUSEUM
61 East Lake Mead Drive
Henderson, Nevada 89015

Dear Dr. Bagley:

Thank you for your recent letter requesting a pair of
my glasses for your museum.

I am enclosing a pair of my old glasses for your most
unusual museum and I wish you every success.

Thanks again and my very best wishes to you and yours.

Love 'n kisses,

Jimmy Durante

JIMMY DURANTE

JD/lt

Enclosure

DOUGLAS FAIRBANKS, JR.

Captain United States Navy 1941-54, Beach Jumpers, World War II

Birth name:	Douglas Elton Fairbanks, Jr.
Born:	December 9, 1909
	New York City, New York
Died:	May 7, 2000 (aged 90)
	New York City, New York
Cause of death:	heart attack
Occupation:	Actor, Naval Officer
Years active:	1916-1997
Spouse(s):	Joan Crawford, Mary Lee Eppling, Vera Shelton
Children:	Daphne Fairbanks, Victoria Fairbanks, Melissa Fairbanks
Parents:	Douglas Fairbanks and Anna Beth Sully

When I was a kid I loved to watch action movies, especially sword fights. Douglas Fairbank Jr. followed in his father's footsteps and accomplished this.

Douglas Elton Fairbanks, Jr. was an American actor and a highly decorated naval officer of World War II, he was a Captain of the Beach Jumpers.

Douglas Fairbanks, Jr. was born in New York City as the only child of actor Douglas Fairbanks and his first wife, Anna Beth Sully. His parents divorced when he was nine years old, and although both remarried, neither had any more children. He lived with his mother in New York, California, Paris and London.

Fairbanks' father was one of cinema's first icons, noted for such swashbuckling adventure films as "The Mark of Zorro" and "Robin Hood" and "The Thief of Bagdad." Largely on the basis of his father's name, Fairbanks, Jr. was given a contract with Paramount Pictures at age 14. After making some undistinguished films, he took to the stage, where he impressed his father, his stepmother, Mary Pickford, and Charlie Chaplin, who encouraged him to continue with acting.

He began his career during the silent film era. He initially played mainly supporting roles in a range of films featuring many of the leading female players of the day.

He was married three times; to Joan Crawford, they were married from 1929 to 1933, Mary Lee Eppling, they were married from 1939 to 1988 until her death, Vera Shelton married from 1991 to 2000 until his death. He has three children; Daphne Fairbanks, Victoria Fairbanks and Melissa Fairbanks.[69]

Melvin J. Bagley

50 EAST 58TH STREET
NEW YORK 22, N. Y.
—
ELDORADO 5-4200

29th November, 1962.

Dr. M. J. Bagley,
Director,
Famous People's Eye Glasses Museum,
61 East Frontier Boulevard,
Henderson, Nevada.

Dear Dr. Bagley,

Mr. Fairbanks saw your kind letter of November 23rd just as he was leaving for Atlanta. He asked me, therefore, if I would thank you on his behalf for writing to him and say how extremely sorry he is that unfortunately he has not kept any of his old eye glasses.

Yours must be a very interesting collection and we wish you every success for it in the future.

Yours sincerely,

Juliette Fowles

Secretary to Mr. Douglas Fairbanks Jr.

206

50 EAST 58TH STREET
NEW YORK, N. Y. 10022
ELDORADO 5-4200

OCTOBER 15, 1971

DR. M. J. BAGLEY
DIRECTOR
FAMOUS PEOPLE'S EYE GLASSES MUSEUM
61 EAST LAKE MEAD DRIVE
HENDERSON, NEVADA 89015

DEAR DR. BAGLEY:

I FOUND AN OLD PAIR OF MY EYEGLASSES WHICH
I AM ENCLOSING HEREWITH AND YOU ARE WELCOME
TO ADD THEM TO YOUR COLLECTION.

SOMETIME, AT YOUR LEISURE, YOU MIGHT SEND
ALONG ANY INFORMATION YOU MAY HAVE ON YOUR
MUSEUM, AS I WOULD LIKE TO HAVE IT FOR MY
COLLECTION.

VERY TRULY YOURS,

DOUGLAS FAIRBANKS

TED MACK
Radio TV Host

Birth name:	William Edward Maguiness
Born:	February 12, 1904
	Greely, Colorado
Died:	July 12, 1976 (aged 72)
	North Tarrytown, New York
Occupation:	Broadcaster, bandleader, musician

> Back in my early days of watching television Ted Mack was the host to any folk that went on to become very famous.

Ted Mack was the host of *Ted Mack and the Original Amateur Hour* on radio and television.

In the late 1920s clarinetist Mack formed a dance band, under his real name. A nightclub owner didn't like "Edward Maguiness" so he changed the bandleader's name to the shorter and snappier "Ted Mack." The name stuck. *The Original Amateur Hour* began on radio in 1934 as *Major Bowes' Amateur Hour* and ran until 1946.

It lasted on radio until 1952 and until 1970 on television, where it ran on all four major networks, ending as a Sunday afternoon CBS staple. A success in the early days of television, the program set the stage for numerous programs seeking talented stars, from *The Gong Show* to *Star Search* to *American Idol* to *America's Got Talent.*

Auditions for the show were generally held in New York's Radio City Music Hall. Those who passed the initial screening were invited to compete on the program, featuring amateurs whose performance were judged by viewers, voting via letters and phone calls. Contestants who won three times earned cash prizes, scholarships, or participation in a traveling stage show associated with the program.

Winners who went on to show business careers included singers Gladys Knight, Ann-Margret, Pat Boone, Raul Julia, Teresa Brewer, Irene Cara, The Rock and Roll Trio and Los Concertinos from Puerto Rico.

Ted Mack and producer Lewis Graham programmed something for everybody. A single broadcast on Easter Sunday, 1959, featured an opera singer, a trumpet sextet, a dulcimer player, a kiddie dance troupe, a young vocalist, a dancer, a rhythm-and-blues combo, a barbershop quartet, and mother-and-son Irish step dancers. Mack's pleasant manner and unflappable calm put many nervous contestants at ease, and he used the same down-to-earth tone for commercials and public-service announcements.

Mack and his wife Ellen had no children but fostered children from Catholic charities at their home.[70]

Melvin J. Bagley

THE ORIGINAL AMATEUR HOUR
INCORPORATED
1270 AVENUE OF THE AMERICAS
NEW YORK, N. Y. 10020

CIRCLE 6-7300

MArch 16th., '72

Dr. M.J. Bagley
61 East Lake Mead Drive
Henderson, Nevada 89015

Dear Sir:

It has taken me a long, long time to answer your request. However, at long last here are the glasses you requested. They are in a rather sad state of repair but they seem to be the only ones I can locate.

Yours must be a very interesting display and if I am ever fortunate enough to be in your vicinity I would like to see it.

With best wishes, I am,

Sincerely,

Ted Mack

Ted Mack

LORETTA LYNN

Birth name:	Loretta Webb
Also known as:	The Coal Miner's Daughter
	The First Lady of Country Music
	The Decca doll
	The Queen of Country Music
Born:	April 14, 1932
	Butcher Hollow, Kentucky, US
Genres	Country, honky-tonk, gospel
Occupations:	Singer, songwriter, author
Instruments:	Vocal, guitar
Years Active:	1960 – present
Labels:	Zero, Decca/MCA, Columbia, Audium, Interscope

> Anybody that followed the early career of Loretta has got to have a great admiration for her accomplishments.

Loretta Lynn, born Loretta Webb April 14, 1932, is an American country-music singer-songwriter and author, born in Butcher Hollow, near Paintsville, Kentucky, to a coal-miner father. At the age of 15 she married, and soon she became pregnant. She moved to Washington state with her husband, Oliver Vanetta Lynn, Jr. married 1926 to 1996, nicknamed "Doo." Their marriage was tumultuous, he had affairs, and she was headstrong, their life together helped to inspire her music.

On their 6 year anniversary, at the age of 21, Lynn's husband bought her a $17 Harmony guitar. She taught herself to play. When she was 24, on her wedding anniversary, he encouraged her to become a singer.

She focused on blue collar women's issues with themes about philandering husbands and persistent mistresses, and pushed boundaries in the conservative genre of country music by singing about birth control "The Pill," repeated childbirth "One's on the Way," double standards for men and women "Rated X," and being widowed by the draft during the Vietnam War "Dear Uncle Sam."

Country music radio stations often refused to play her music, banning nine of her songs. But Loretta pushed on to become "The First Lady of Country Music." Her best-selling 1976 autobiography was made into an Academy Award-winning film, *Coal Miners Daughter,* starring Sissy Spacek and Tommy Lee Jones, in 1980.

Her most recent album, *Van Lear Rose,* was released in 2004, produced by Jack White, and it topped the country album charts. Loretta has received numerous awards in country and American music. For over 50 years Loretta has been performing and was honored in 2010 at the Country Music Awards for her stellar career. Loretta has been a member of The Grand Ole Opry for 50 years since joining on September 25, 1962.[71]

Loretta Lynn ENTERPRISES, Inc.

| 1511 SIGLER ST. | • | NASHVILLE, TENNESSEE 37203 | • | 615/259-2021 |

January 27, 1975

Dr. M. J. Bagley, Director
Famous People's Eye Glasses Museum
Henderson, Nevada

Dear Mr. Bagley:

Here's a pair of my old sunglasses. I am happy to send them to
you for your museum.

Thanks for thinking of me.

Your friend,

Loretta Lynn

CARL ALBERT

Born:	May 10, 1908
	McAlester, Oklahoma
Died:	February 4, 2000 (aged 91)
	McAlester, Oklahoma
Political party:	Democratic
Alma mater	University of Oklahoma
	St Peter's College, Oxford
Profession:	Lawyer

When I received these glasses, I felt quite flattered that he would send me his first glasses he ever owned. He is the father of Medicare.

Carl Bert Albert was a lawyer and a Democratic American politician from Oklahoma.

Albert represented the southeastern portion of Oklahoma Congressional District 3, as a Democrat for 30 years, starting in 1947. He is best known for his service as Speaker of the United States House of Representatives from 1971 to 1977. At 5 feet 4 inches tall, Albert was often affectionately known as the "Little Giant from Little Dixie," and held the highest political office of any Oklahoman in American history.

As Majority Leader, Albert was a key figure in advancing the Democratic legislative agenda in the House, particularly with health care legislation. Medicare, the federal program of hospital insurance for persons 65 and older, was initially proposed by the Kennedy Administration as an amendment to the Social Security program. Albert knew the bill had insufficient Congressional support for passage due to the opposition of ten key Republicans and with key southern Democrats. He advised President Kennedy to seek Senate passage of the measure first. Albert calculated that the Senate should bring it to the House as a conference and committee report on their own welfare bill, instead of trying direct introduction into the Houses.

Albert's efforts, although well-planned on behalf of the Medicare bill' were not successful at that time. After the Kennedy assassination, Albert worked to change House rules so that the majority Democrats would have greater influence on the final decisions of Congress under President Lyndon B Johnson. The changes included more majority leverage over the House Rules Committee, and stronger majority membership influence in the House Ways and Means Committee. With these changes in place, Albert was able to push through the Medicare bill, known as the Social Security Act of 1965, and he shepherded other pieces of Johnson's Great Society program through Congress.[72]

The Speaker's Rooms
U.S. House of Representatives
Washington, D. C. 20515

January 29, 1975

Dr. M. J. Bagley
Director
Famous People's Eye Glasses Museum
61 East Lake Mead Drive
Henderson, Nevada 89015

Dear Dr. Bagley:

Thank you for your letter requesting a pair of my eye glasses to be added to the collection at the Famous People's Eye Glasses Museum. Under separate cover, I am sending the first pair of eye glasses I owned which are approximately twenty three years old. I was happy to make this contribution to the museum.

With every good wish, I am

Sincerely,

Carl Albert

The Speaker

CA/tk

HUGH DOWNS

Birth name:	Hugh Malcolm Downs
Born:	February 14, 1921
	Akron, Ohio, US
Occupation:	Television broadcaster, host, producer, author
Years active:	1945–1999
Spouse:	Ruth Shaheen (m. 1944)
Children:	1

This letter from Mr. Downs illustrates a strange phenomena in vision. The pupil of the eye reacts to light, like a shutter of a camera it gets small in bright light and large in dim light. When people get older, the pupil forgets how to do this and stays small all the time. In certain refractive cases this creates a focus at all distances. In Mr. Down's case, he must have had just the right refractive error to fall in this category.

Hugh Malcolm Downs is a long-time American broadcaster, television host, news anchor, TV producer, author, game show host and music composer. He is perhaps best known for his role as co-host of the NBC News program *"Today"* from 1962 to 1971, and anchor of the ABC News magazine *20/20* from 1975 to 1999. In addition, he's served as announcer/sidekick for *Tonight Starring Jack Paar*, hosted the PBS talk show *Over Easy*, and co-host of the syndicated talk show *Not for Women Only*.

Downs was a special consultant to the United Nations for refugee problems from 1961 to 1964 and served as Chairman of the Board of the United States Committee for UNICEF.

Downs wrote a column for Science Digest during the 1960s. He was Science Consultant to Westinghouse Laboratories and the Ford Foundation and an elected member of the National Academy of Science. He is a Board of Governors member of the National Space Society and was a longtime president and chairman of the predecessor National Space Institute. The asteroid 71000 Hughdowns is named after him.

The auditorium of Shawnee High School in Lima, Ohio and the Hugh Downs School of Human Communication of Arizona State University in Tempe, Arizona, are named in his honor.

Downs has expressed public praise for many libertarian viewpoints. He opposes the U.S. "war on drugs." He did several pieces about the war on drugs and hemp. On his last 20/20 he was asked if he had any opinions of his own that he would like to express: he responded that marijuana should be legalized.[73]

HUGH DOWNS

January 30, 1975

Dr. M.J. Bagley, Director
Famous People's Eye Glasses Museum
61 East Lake Mead Drive
Henderson, Nevada 89015

Dear Dr. Bagley:

The pair of glasses I'm sending for the Famous
People's Eye Glasses Museum represents what
might be an interesting bit of medical history:

I started wearing glasses about a quarter of a
century ago and in the last 10 years have gotten
successively milder prescriptions until now I do
not need glasses for anything. This pair
represents about two or three prescriptions back
and I wore them between 1960 and 1964. Now,
neither my pilot's license nor my driver's license
are marked to require glasses. And while my vision
is not quite perfect it has gone back to the way it
was when I was in my teens - very nearly 100%.

Yours sincerely,

Hugh Downs

HD:jf
Enc.

ROGER STAUBACH

Born:	February 5, 1942
Place of birth:	Cincinnati, Ohio
Position(s):	Quarterback
College:	U. S. Naval Academy
AFL Draft:	1964/Round 10
Drafted by:	Kansas City Chiefs
NFL Draft:	1964/ Round 10/ Pick 129
Drafted by:	Dallas Cowboys

I understand now why Roger Stauback did not need glasses for watching him play, it was almost like eyes on the side of his head.

Roger Thomas Staubach is former star National Football League quarterback and current businessman.

After his required service in the United States Navy, including a tour of duty in Vietnam, Staubach joined the Dallas Cowboys in 1969. He played with the club during five seasons in which they played in the Super Bowl, four as the primary starting quarterback. He led the Cowboys to victories in Super Bowl VI and Super Bowl XII. Staubach was named Most Valuable Player of Super Bowl VI, becoming the first of four players to win the Heisman Trophy and Super Bowl MVP-Jim Plunkett, Marcus Allen, and Desmond Howard are the other three. He was named to the Pro Bowl six times during his eleven-year NFL career.[74]

dallas cowboys football club

January 30, 1975

Dr. M. J. Bagley
Director
Famous People's Eye Glasses Museum
61 East Lake Mead Drive
Henderson, Nevada 89015

Dear Dr. Bagley:

Thank you for your letter regarding adding
a pair of glasses to your Museum.

I am sorry that I won't be able to help
out, but I have never worn glasses.

Sincerely,

Roger Staubach

RS:rc

6116 N. Central Expressway ● Dallas, Texas 75206 ● Area Code 214/369-3211
(Executive Offices ● Area Code 214/369-8000)

WILLIAM REHNQUIST

Birth name:	William Donald Rehnquist
Born:	October 1, 1924
	Milwaukee, Wisconsin
Died:	September 3, 2005 (age 80)
	Arlington, Virginia, US
Spouse:	Nan Cornell
Alma Mater:	Stanford University, Harvard University, Stanford Law School
Religion:	Lutheran
	Sixteenth Chief Justice of the United States, 1986 to 2005
Appointed by:	Ronald Reagan
	Associated Justice of the Supreme Court of the United States 1972 to 1988
Appointed by:	Richard Nixon
	United States Assistant Attorney General for the Office of Legal Counsel
	In office1969–1971
President:	Richard Nixon

William Hubbs Rehnquist was an American lawyer, jurist and political figure who served as an Associated Justice of the Supreme Court of The United States and later as the 16th Chief Justice of the United States. Considered a conservative, Rehnquist favored conception of federalism that emphasized the Tenth Amendments reservation of powers to the states. Under this view of federalism, The Supreme Court of the United States for the first time since the 1930s struck down an Act of Congress as exceeding its power under The Commerce Clause.

Rehnquist served as Chief Justice for nearly 19 years, making him the fourth longest serving Chief Justice after John Marshall, Roger Taney and Melville Tanner and the longest-serving Chief Justice who had previously served as an Associate Justice. The last 11 years of Rehnquists term as Chief Justice (1994–2005) marked the second-longest tenure of a single unchanging roster of the Supreme Court. He is the eighth longest-serving justice in Supreme Court history.

He married Natalie Cornell on August 29, 1953. She died on October 17, 1991, after suffering from ovarian cancer. They had three children, James, Janet and Nancy and nine grandchildren.

He purchased a home in Greensboro, Vermont, where he spent the summer court recess with his family.[75]

Melvin J. Bagley

Supreme Court of the United States
Washington, D. C. 20543

CHAMBERS OF
JUSTICE WILLIAM H. REHNQUIST

January 31, 1975

Dr. M. J. Bagley, Director
Famous People's Eye Glasses Museum
61 East Lake Mead Drive
Henderson, Nevada 89015

Dear Dr. Bagley:

I have received your letter of January 8th asking for
a pair of my old glasses. I don't have one available right
now, but if in the future I get some new glasses I will try
to remember to send you the old ones.

Sincerely,

[signature]

SPIRO AGNEW

39th Vice President of the United States

Birth name:	Spiro Theodore Agnew
Born:	November 9, 1918
	Baltimore, Maryland
Died:	September 17, 1996
	(aged 77)
	Berlin, Maryland
Resting place:	Dulaney Valley Memorial Gardens
	Timonium Maryland
Political Party:	Republican
Spouse(s):	Judy Agnew
Children:	Pamela Agnew, James Rand Agnew

> Spiro T. Agnew sticks in my mind, as well as people in his generation, as one of the only Vice Presidents in American history to resign. Although, his glasses in my museum are the only ones belonging to a Vice President of America.

Spiro Theodore Agnew was an American politician who served as the 39th Vice President of the United States from 1969 to 1973, serving under President Richard Nixon.

Agnew was a graduate of Johns Hopkins University and University of Baltimore School of Law. He was drafted into the United States Army in 1941, serving as an officer during World War II, and was recalled for service during the Korean War in 1950. He worked as an aide for U.S. Representative James Devereux before he was appointed to the Baltimore County Board of Zoning Appeals in 1957. He lost an election for the Baltimore City Circuit Court in 1960, but was later elected Baltimore County Executive in 1962. In 1966 Agnew was elected the 55th Governor of Maryland, defeating Democratic opponent George P. Mahoney. He was the first Greek American to hold the position, serving from 1967 to 1969.

On October 10, 1973, Agnew was allowed to plead no contest to a single charge that he had failed to report $29,500 of income received in 1967, with the condition that he resign the office of Vice President. Nixon replaced him by appointing then House Minority Leader Gerald R. Ford to the office of Vice President.

Agnew is the only Vice President in United States history to resign because of criminal charges. Ten years after leaving office, in January 1983, Agnew paid the State of Maryland nearly $270,000 as a result of a civil suit that stemmed from the bribery allegations.

Married to Judy Agnew, together they have four children Pamela, Susan, Kimberly, and James.[76]

PATHLITE, INC.

International Trade

11-A VILLAGE GREEN
CROFTON, MARYLAND 21113

TELEPHONE 301 721-7277   February 5, 1975   TELEX 892769

Dr. M. J. Bagley
Director
Famous People's Eye Glasses Museum
61 East Lake Mead Drive
Henderson, Nevada   89015

Dear Dr. Bagley:

     Mr. Agnew is travelling out of the country; however, when I
spoke with him about your request, he asked me to send you the
enclosed pair of his old glasses.

     Kind regards.

                Sincerely,

                Mary Ellen Warner
                Secretary to
                Spiro T. Agnew

Enclosure: one pair eye glasses

MELVYN DOUGLAS

Birth name:	Melvyn Eduard Hesselberg
Born:	April 5, 1901
	Macon, Georgia, US
Died:	August 4, 1981 (aged 80)
	New York City, New York, US
Occupation:	Actor
Years active:	1927-1981
Spouse(s):	Rosalind Hightower, Helen Gahagan
	2 sons, 1 daughter

Douglas was born in Macon, Georgia, the son of Lena Priscilla Shackelford and Edward Gregory Hesselberg, a concert pianist and composer. His father was a Jewish immigrant from Riga, Latvia, then part of Russia. His mother, a native of Tennessee, was Protestant and a Mayflower descendant. His maternal grandfather, George Shackelford, was a General and Civil War veteran.

Douglas, in his autobiography, *See You at the Movies* in 1987, wrote that he was unaware of his Jewish background until later in his youth: "I did not learn about the non-Christian part of my heritage until my early teens," as his parents preferred to hide his Jewish heritage.

Though his father taught music at a succession of colleges in the U.S. and Canada, Douglas never graduated from high school. He took the surname of his maternal grandmother and became known as Melvyn Douglas.

Douglas developed his acting skills in Shakespearean repertory while in his teens and with stock companies in Sioux City, Iowa, Evansville, Indiana, Madison, Winsconsin and Detroit, Michigan. He established an outdoor theatre in Chicago.

Melvyn Douglas was married briefly to artist Rosalind Hightower, and they had one child Melvyn Gregory Hasselberg. In 1931 Douglas married actress-politician Helen Gahagan. He was married to Helen until her death in 1980. Melvyn Douglas died a year later in 1981 at the age of 80 from pneumonia and cardiac complications in New York City.

He won two Academy Awards; one in 1963 for Best Supporting Actor for the film *Hud*. In 1979, he won for Best Supporting Actor for the film *Being There*.[77]

MELVYN DOUGLAS

50 RIVERSIDE DRIVE   NEW YORK, N. Y. 10024

February 5, 1975

Dear Dr. Bagley:

This is indeeda belated reply to your letter,
but Mr. and Mrs. Douglas have been away from
New York since mid-December and I have only now
finished struggling with asthma and a lingering
cold.

I expect the Douglas' to return to the city early
in April. I will, of course, hold your letter for
his return and if he does have a pair of glasses to
send, I am sure he will.

Sincerely,

Nan Stevens
secretary

Dr. M. J. Bagley
Director
Famous People's Eye Glasses Museum
61 East Lake Mead Drive
Henderson, Nevada 89015

DON MCLEAN

Birth name:	Donald McLean
Born:	October 2, 1945
	New Rochelle, New York
Genres:	Folk, folk rock
Occupations:	Singer-songwriter, musician
Instruments:	Vocals, guitar, banjo, piano
Years active:	1969-present
Labels:	United Artists, EMI America

"Good old boys drinking whiskey and rye", what clever words, written by a very clever Don McLean.

Donald "Don" McLean is an American singer- songwriter. He is most famous for the 1971 album American Pie, containing the songs "American Pie" and "Vincent."

McLean's grandfather and father were also named Donald McLean. The Buccis, the family of McLean's mother, Elizabeth, came from Abruzzo in central Italy. They left Italy and settled in Port Chester, New York, at the end of the 19th century. He has other extended family in Los Angeles and Boston.

As a teenager, McLean became interested in folk music, particularly the Weavers' 1955 recording At Carnegie Hall. Childhood asthma meant that McLean missed long periods of school, particularly music lessons, and although he slipped back in his studies, his love of music was allowed to flourish. By age 16 he had bought his first guitar and began making contacts in the music business, becoming friends with folk singer Erik Darling, a latter-day member of the Weavers. McLean recorded his first studio sessions, with singer Lisa Kindred, while still in prep school.

McLean graduated from Iona Preparatory School in 1963, and briefly attended Villanova University, dropping out after four months. While at Villanova he became friends with singer and songwriter Jim Croce.

McLean became associated with famed folk music agent Harold Leventhal for several months before teaming up with personal manager Herb Gart for 18 years. For the next six years he performed at venues and events. McLean attended night school at Iona College and received a bachelor's degree in business administration in 1968. He turned down a scholarship to Columbia University Graduate School in favor of becoming resident singer at Caffe Lena in Saratoga Springs, New York.

In 1968, with the help of a grant from the New York State Council on the Arts, McLean began reaching a wider public, with visits to towns up and down the Hudson River.[78]

February, 19, 1975

Gentlemen;

It seemed so weird to even think about an eyeglass museum, that I'm sending a pair. I bought these in England, which may explain them.

Sincerely,

Don McLean

RYAN O'NEAL

Birth name:	Charles Patrick Ryan O'Neal, Jr.
Born:	April 20, 1941
	Los Angeles, California, US
Education:	University High School
	Munich American High School
Occupation:	Actor
Years active:	1960–Present
Spouse(s):	Joanna Moore, Leigh Taylor-Young,
Partner(s):	Farrah Fawcett
Children:	Tatum O'Neal, Griffin O'Neal, Charles Patrick Ryan O'Neal III,
	Redmond James Fawcett O'Neal
Parents:	Charles O'Neal and Patricia O'Neal

This is strange while I got a letter from Ryan O'Neal saying he did not have a glasses to send me but on a later date he send me a pair of his glasses. This only happen once in a while.

Charles Patrick Ryan O'Neal, Jr. also known as Ryan O'Neal, is an American television and film actor.

O'Neal trained as an amateur boxer before beginning his career in acting in 1960. In 1964, he landed the role of Rodney Harrington on the ABC nighttime soap opera *Peyton Place*. The series was an instant hit and boosted

O'Neal's career. He later found success in films, most notably *Paper Moon* (1973), Stanley Kubrick's *Barry Lyndon* (1975), *A Bridge Too Far* (1977), and *Love Story* (1970), for which he received Academy Award and Golden Globe nominations as Best Actor. Since 2007, he has had a recurring role in the TV series *Bones*.

O'Neal has been married twice and has four children. His eldest child, Tatum, is an Academy Award–winning actress. He was also in a long-term relationship with actress Farrah Fawcett from 1979 to 1997, and from 2001 until her death in 2009.[79]

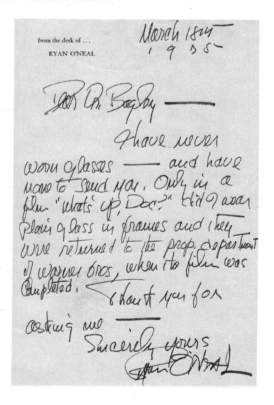

HENRY KISSINGER

56th United States Secretary of State

Birth name:	Heinz Alfred Kissinger
Born:	May 27, 1923
	Furth, Bavaria, Germany
Political party:	Republican
Spouse(s):	Ann Fleischer (1949-1964)
	Nancy Maginnes (1974-present)
Alma mater:	Harvard University
Religion:	Judaism

Henry Kissinger has remain through the years as the most brilliant understanding of Foreign Policy Politician still seek his advice.

Heinz Alfred Kissinger is a German-born American writer, political scientist, diplomat, and businessman. A recipient of the Nobel Peace Prize, he served as National Security Advisor and later concurrently as Secretary of State in the administrations of Presidents Richard Nixon and Gerald Ford. After his term, his opinion was still sought by some subsequent US presidents and other world leaders.

His father Louis Kissinger was a schoolteacher and his mother Paula Stern was a homemaker. Kissinger has a younger brother Walter Kissinger. As a young boy, Kissinger enjoyed playing soccer, and even played for the youth side of his favorite club and one of the nation's best clubs at the time. In 1938, fleeing Nazi persecution, his family moved to London, England before arriving in New York.

Kissinger first married Ann Fleischer, with whom he had two children Elizabeth and David. They divorced in 1964. Ten years later, he married Nancy Maginnes. They now live in Kent, Connecticut and New York City.

Secretary of State Kissinger and Le Du Tho were jointly awarded the 1973 Nobel Peace Prize for their work on the Paris Peace Accords which prompted the withdrawal of American Forces from the Vietnam War. In 1976 Kissinger became the first honorary member of the Harlem Globetrotters. On January 13, 1977, Kissinger received the Presidential Medal of Freedom from President Gerald Ford. In 1980 Kissinger won the National Book Award in History for the first volume of his memoirs, *The White House Years*. He received numerous awards, honors and associations.

Kissinger played a prominent role in United States foreign policy between 1969 and 1977. During this period, he pioneered the policy of détente with the Soviet Union, orchestrated the opening of relations with the People's Republic of China, and negotiated the Paris Peace Accords, ending American involvement in the Vietnam War.

Kissinger is still considered an influential public figure. He is the founder and chairman of Kissinger Associates, an international consulting firm.[80]

Celebrity Sighting

DEPARTMENT OF STATE

Washington, D.C. 20520

April 8, 1975

Dr. M. J. Bagley
61 East Lake Mead Drive
Henderson, Nevada 89015

Dear Dr. Bagley:

Secretary Kissinger has asked me to reply to your
letter asking that he send you a pair of glasses
for your museum.

The Secretary regrets that he cannot respond posi-
tively to your request. He believes that because
he receives so many similarly deserving appeals, he
cannot fairly respond to one and not to the others.
However, he sends you his best wishes for the success of your very worthwhile project.

Sincerely yours,

Carol C. Laise
Assistant Secretary
for Public Affairs

ANWAR SADAT

**President of the Arab Republic of Egypt,
Formerly President of the United Arab Republic**

Birth name:	Muhammad Anwar El-Sadat
Born:	25 December 1918
	El Monufia, Egypt
Died:	6 October 1981 Aged 62
	Cairo, Egypt
Nationality:	Egyptian
Spouses:	Ehsan Madi and Jehan Sadat
Religion:	Sunni Islam

I could not believe that just a week after we received not one, but two pairs of glasses, from Anwar Sadat, he was assassinated. In my experience I have found that it is almost impossible to get any glasses from anyone who has already died.

Anwar El Sadat was the third President of Egypt, serving from 15 October 1970 until his assassination by Fundamentalist Army officers on 6 October 1981. In his eleven years as president, he changed Egypt's direction, departing from some of the economic and political principles of Nasserism by re-instituting the multi-party system and launching the Infitah Economic Policy.

Sadat was a senior member of the Free Officers Group that overthrew Farouk I in the Egyptian Revolution of 1952 and a close confidant of President Gamal Abdul Nasser, whom he succeeded as President in 1970. As president, he led Egypt in the October War of 1973 to re-acquire Egyptian territory lost to Israel in the 1967 Six-Day War, making him a hero in Egypt and, for a time, the wider Arab World. Afterwards, he engaged in negotiations with Israel, culminating in the Egypt-Israel Peace Treaty, it won him the Nobel Peace Prize but also made him unpopular among some Arabs, resulting in a temporary suspension of Egypt's membership in the Arab League and eventually his assassination.

Vice-President Hosni Mubarak succeeded President Sadat as head of state.

On 6 October 1981, Sadat was assassinated during the annual victory parade held in Cairo to celebrate Egypt's crossing of the Suez Canal. Sadat and eleven others were killed, including the Cuban Ambassador, an Omani general, a Coptic Orthodox bishop and Samir Helmy, head of Egypt's head of the Central Auditing Agency (CAA). Twenty-eight were wounded, including Vice President Hosni Mubarak, Irish Defence Minister James Tully, and four US military liaison officers.

President Sadat of Egypt has died after being shot by gunmen who opened fire as he watched the eighth anniversary of the Yom Kippur War with Israel as Field Marshal of the Armed Forces.

He had taken the salute, laid a wreath and was watching a display from the Egyptian Air Force when two grenades exploded. Gunmen then leapt from a military truck in front of the presidential reviewing stand and ran towards the spectators, raking officials with automatic gunfire. Despite typically large numbers of security personnel for the ceremonial occasion, eyewitnesses say the attackers were able to keep shooting for well over a minute.

By the time the president's bodyguards returned fire at least ten people lay seriously injured or dead inside the stand. Security forces then shot and killed two of the attackers and overpowered the rest, as crowds of military and civilian spectators scrambled for cover. President Sadat was airlifted by helicopter to a military hospital. He is believed to have died about two hours later. The precision with which the attack was coordinated has prompted suspicions that the attackers benefited from high-level intelligence and support. A group calling itself the Independent Organization for the Liberation of Egypt says it carried out the attack but the claim has not been verified.

Reaction to President's Sadat's death has been mixed. President Reagan condemned Anwar Sadat's death as an act of infamy. He said: "America has lost a great friend, the world has lost a great statesman, and mankind has lost a champion of peace." But many have been celebrating the news.

While in Libya, Tripoli radio said every tyrant has an end, as thousands took to the streets of the capital in jubilation. Neither has the Palestinian Liberation Organization condemned the assassination. Nabil Ramlawi, a PLO official, said: "We were expecting this end of President Sadat because we are sure he was against the interests of his people, the Arab Nations and the Palestinian People."

President Sadat was the first Arab leader to recognize the State of Israel since its creation in 1948. Although popular in the West for his efforts at rapprochement with Israel, his policies dismayed much of the Arab World. Under President Sadat, Egypt signed the Camp David accords with Israel in 1978 outlining "the framework for peace in the Middle East." This included limited autonomy for Palestinians. [81]

PHILIP KNIGHT WRIGLEY

Birth name:	Philip Knight Wrigley
Born:	December 5, 1894
	Chicago, Illinois
Died:	April 12, 1977
Owner:	Wm. Wrigley Jr. Company
	Chicago Cubs
Father:	William Wrigley Jr.
Son:	William Wrigley III

Philip Knight Wrigley also called P.K. or Phil was an American chewing gum manufacturer and executive in Major League Baseball, inheriting both those roles as the quiet son of his much more flamboyant father, William Wrigley Jr. In 1912, Wrigley founded the Lincoln Park Gun Club with Oscar F. Mayer, Sewell Avery, and other prominent Chicagoans.

When his father died in 1932. Philip presided over the Wm. Wrigley Jr. Company, and also the family hobby, the Chicago Cubs, as owner until his death. He passed the title of Wm. Wrigley Jr. Company President to his son William Wrigley III in 1961.

While the gum industry prospered, the Cubs grew less competitive over the decades. After an appearance in the 1945 World Series, they only had seven winning seasons in the next 32 years, including 16 straight losing seasons from 1947 to 1962. In 1961 he abolished the traditional field management and coaching structure and instead hired a "College of Coaches". This anticipated the specialization of coaches that is taken for granted nowadays. His one mistake, was not having a manager. Instead, he opted to have the various coaches as a "head coach." Without firm and consistent leadership, the Cubs continued to languish in the standings, despite having Cubs greats Ron Santo, Ernie Banks and Billy Williams on the roster. In 1966 he hired Leo Durocher as the manager.

During World War II, Wrigley founded the All-American Girls Professional Baseball League as a promotional sideline to maintain interest in baseball as the World War II military draft was depleting major-league rosters of first-line players. The AAGPBL was immortalized in the 1992 film, A League of Their Own.

After PK and his wife died, their son William III took over both enterprises. The Cubs were sold to the Tribune Company in 1981, ending over 60 years of Wrigley association with the team, save the name of the ballpark itself, which remains Wrigley Field.

Continuing the environmental stewardship of his father, he established the Catalina Island Conservancy in 1972, and donated his family's ownership of most of Santa Catalina Island, 26 miles off the coast of Los Angeles, to the Catalina Island Conservancy.[82]

Julie Ann Burns

ATTORNEY AT LAW

1600 WRIGLEY BUILDING • 410 NORTH MICHIGAN AVENUE • CHICAGO, ILLINOIS 60611

January 16, 1981

Dr. M. J. Bagley, Director
Famous People's Eye Glasses Museum
61 East Lake Mead Drive
Box 775
Henderson, Nevada 89015

Dear Dr. Bagley:

Your letter of January 15, 1981,
addressed to Mr. Philip K. Wrigley has been
received.

I am one of the attorneys representing
the Estate of Philip K. Wrigley. I regret to
inform you that Mr. Wrigley passed away in 1977,
and therefore, we will be unable to help you
with your request.

Sincerely,

Julie A. Burns

JAB:tms

MARGARET THATCHER
Prime Minister of the United Kingdom

Birth name:	Margaret Hilda Roberts
Born:	13 October 1925
	Grantham, England
Died:	8 April 2013 (aged 87)
	London, England
Political party:	Conservative
Spouse(s):	Dennis Thatcher
	(m. 1951-2003 his death)
Children:	Carol Thatcher
	Mark Thatcher
Alma mater	Summerville College, Oxford Inns of Court
Profession:	Chemist
	Lawyer
Religion:	Church of England and Methodist

Wow, here is another reply form a very famous
person who apparently never needed glasses.

Margaret Hilda Thatcher, Baroness Thatcher, was a
British politician who was the Prime Minister of The
United Kingdom from 1979 to 1990 and The Leader
of the Conservative Party from 1975 to 1990. She was
the longest-serving British Prime Minister of the 20th
century and is the only woman and only scientist. She
was also called the Iron Lady, a nickname that became

associated with her uncompromising politics and leadership style. As Prime Minister, she implemented policies that have come to be known as Thatcherism.

Originally a research chemist before becoming a barrister, Thatcher was elected Member of Parliament for Finchley in 1959. Edward Heath appointed her Secretary of State for Education and Science in his 1970 government. In 1975, Thatcher defeated Heath in the Conservative Party leadership election to become Leader of the Opposition and became the first women to lead a major political party in The United Kingdom. She became Prime Minister after winning the 1979 general election.

Upon moving into 10 Downing Street, Thatcher introduced a series of political and economic initiatives intended to reverse high unemployment and Britain's struggles in the wake of the Winter of Discontent and an ongoing recession. Her political philosophy and economic policies emphasized deregulation, particularly of the financial sector, flexible labor markets, the privatization of state-owned companies, and reducing the power and influence of trade unions. She won re-election after re-election.

She married Denis Thatcher in 1951. They have two children, Carol Thatcher and Mark Thatcher.[83]

10 DOWNING STREET

From the Private Secretary　　　　　　20 January,1981

Dear Dr Bagley.

　　　　　The Prime Minister has asked me to thank
you for your letter of 15 January asking her to
contribute to your 'Famous People's Eye Glasses
Museum'. Unfortunately we are unable to help
you as Mrs Thatcher has never worn glasses.

　　　With best wishes.

Yours sincerely,

Caroline Stephens

Dr M J Bagley

MAURICE STRONG

Birth name:	Maurice F. Strong
Born:	April 29, 1929
	Oak Lake, Manitoba, Canada

After receiving a letter from Geneva, another from London, then another from Arizona, Maurice Strong finally sent me a pair of glasses, as promised.

Maurice F. Strong, is a Canadian entrepreneur and a former undersecretary general of the United Nations. Strong's first name is pronounced Morris with the accent on the first syllable.

Strong had his start as an entrepreneur in the Alberta oil patch and was president of Power Corporation of Canada until 1966. In the early 1970s he was secretary general of the United Nations Conference on the Human Environment and then became the first executive director of the United Nations Environment Programme. He returned to Canada to become chief executive officer of Petro-Canada from 1976 to 1978. He headed Ontario Hydro, one of North America's largest power utilities, was national president and chairman of the Extension Committee of the World Alliance of YMCAs, and headed American Water Development Incorporated. He served as a commissioner of the World Commission on Environment and Development in 1986 and is recognized by the International Union for Conservation of Nature as a leader in the international environmental movement.

He was president of the council of the University for Peace from 1998 to 2006. Today Strong is an active honorary professor at Peking University and honorary chairman of its Environmental Foundation. He is chairman of the advisory board for the Institute for Research on Security and Sustainability for Northeast Asia.[84]

Melvin J. Bagley

M. F. Strong

January 22, 1981

Dr. M. J. Bagley
Director
Famous People's Eye Glasses Museum
61 East Lake Mead Drive
Box 775
Henderson
Nevada 89015
U.S.A.

Dear Dr. Bagley:

Would you kindly take note that in the future all
mail addressed to Mr. Maurice F. Strong in Geneva
should be sent to the following address:

> International Energy Development
> Corporation
> 18, rue le Corbusier
>
> 1208 Geneva
>
> Tel: (22) 47 74 47
> Tlx: 23710 (iedc ch)

Yours sincerely,

Jacqueline Forbes

J. N. Forbes
Secretary

P. O. Box 29008
Phoenix, AZ 85038

August 14, 1981

Dr. M. J. Bagley
Director
Famous People's Eye
  Glasses Museum
61 East Lake Mead Drive
Box 775
Henderson, NE 89015

Dear Dr. Bagley:

As indicated in my letter of February 17, 1981, I am
pleased to enclose a pair of my eye glasses for your
Museum.

Yours sincerely,

Maurice F. Strong

M. F. Strong

32 St. James's Street
London SW1A 1HD, England

February 17, 1981

Dr. M. J. Bagley
Director
Famous People's Eye
  Glasses Museum
61 East Lake Mead Drive
Box 775
Henderson, Nevada 89015

Dear Dr. Bagley:

Many thanks for your letter of January 15 and your invitation for me to add a pair of my eye glasses to your "Famous People's Eye Glasses Museum". I would be pleased to do this. However, as I have only recently begun to wear glasses I do not have an extra pair I can contribute at the moment. I will do so as soon as I have a pair available in the future.

Let me say, in the meantime, how much I appreciate the compliment you pay me in extending this invitation.

Yours sincerely,

Maurice Strong

GODDARD LIEBERSON

Born:	April 5, 1911
Died:	May 29, 1977 (aged 66)
	Manhattan, New York
Spouse(s)	Vera Zorina (m.1946-1977)

When we got these glasses from Mr. Lieberson's wife, I thought it was very unusual. This was one of the rare cases that we received glasses from someone who had already passed away.

Goddard Lieberson was the president of Columbia Records from 1956 to 1971, and again from 1973 to 1975. He became president of the Recording Industry Association of America in 1964. He was also a composer, and studied with George Frederick McKay, at the University of Washington.

He married actress and dancer Vera Zorina from 1946 until his death in 1977. They had two sons: Peter Lieberson, a composer, and Jonathan Lieberson.

Before becoming president of the company, Lieberson was responsible for Columbia's introduction of the long-playing record. The LP was particularly well-suited to Columbia's long-established classical repertoire, as recorded by the Philadelphia Orchestra under Eugene Ormandy and the New York Philharmonic Orchestra

conducted by Artur Rodziñski, Dmitri Mitropoubos, and
Leonard Bernstein.

He was promoted to president of Columbia Records
from 1956 to 1971 and again from 1973 to 1975.

He died of cancer in New York City on May 29,
1977, aged 66.

Lieberson's recordings at Columbia, were influential.

In addition to documenting the musical performances
of the 1950s, 1960s, and 1970s, Lieberson also produced
notable studio cast recordings of musicals of the 1930s
and 1940s, such as "Pal Joey" and "The Boys from
Syracuse," for which cast albums had not been made.[85]

LILI KRAUS

Birth name:	Lili Kraus
Born:	April 3, 1903
	Budapest, Hungary
Died:	November 6, 1986
	Asheville, North Carolina
Genre:	Classical Pianist
Nationality:	Hungarian

> I always loved it when we got glasses accompanied by a letter, written by the person that has worn the glasses. Some of the letters were were just plain, and to the point but Lili Kraus's letter was classical, just like the music she plays.

Lili Kraus was a Hungarian-born pianist. Her father was from Czech Lands, and her mother from an assimilated Jewish Hungarian family.

She enrolled at the Franz Liszt Academy of Music, and at the age of 17 entered the Budapest conservatory where she studied with Artur Schnabel, Zoltán Kodaly, and Bela Bartok. In the 1930s, she continued her studies with Severin Eisenberger, Eduard Steuermann in Vienna and Arthur Schnabel in Berlin, who focused her interest in the classical tradition.

Lili Kraus became known as a specialist in Mozart and Beethoven. Her early chamber music performances and recording with violinist Szymon Goldberg helped gain the critical acclaim that launched her international career. In the 1930s, she toured Europe, Japan, Australia and South Africa, in 1940, Kraus embarked on a tour of Asia where, while in Java, she and her family were captured and interned in a concentration camp by the Japanese until 1943.

After the war, she settled in New Zealand, became a British citizen and resumed her career, teaching and touring extensively. In the early 1950s she performed the entire Beethoven sonata cycle with violinist Henri Temianka. From 1967 to 1983, she taught as artist-in-residence at Texas Christian University in Fort Worth. After that she made her home in Asheville, North Carolina, where she died in 1986.

Her husband was Jewish, later converted to Catholicism, Austrian philosopher and patron Otto Mandl.[86]

LILI KRAUS

The Hill House,
Celo Farm, Rt. 5,
Burnsville, NC 28714
704/675-4439

January 25, 1981

Dr. M. J. Bagley, Director
Famous People's Eye Glasses Museum
61 East Lake Mead Drive
Box 775
Henderson, Nevada 89015

Dear Dr. Bagley:

It will never cease to amuse me what new ways will be
created to focus attention and obtain amusement.

If I would like to and above all, if I would have the time,
I would make up a glorious story accompanying these glasses.

"Dichtung und Wahrheit" is not better - or not much - than
"Dichtung und Unwahrheit," so I would love to serve you.

Thus I can only wish that my spectacles will fill the
function you imagine and require them to have.

Cordial wishes for a happy 1981.

Yours,

Lili Kraus

Mme. Lili Kraus

LK/djd

PETER BOGDANOVICH

Born: July 30, 1929
                     Kingston, New York, US
Spouse(s):   Polly Platt and Louise Stratten
Partner(s):   Cybill Shepherd

> We received several pairs of glasses, but the number that we received' compared to the number of letters sent, was very small. A friend of mine suggested that we include the phrase "regardless of their condition" to the request.

Peter Bodanovich is an American film historian, director, writer, actor, producer and critic. He was part of the wave of "New Hollywood" directors, which included William Friedkin, Brian De Palma, George Lucas, Martin Scorsese, Michael Cimino and Francis Ford Coppola. His most critically acclaimed film is *The Last Picture Show*.

Much of the inspiration which led Bogdanovich to his cinematic creations came from early viewings of the film *Citizen Kane*. In an interview with Robert K. Elder, author of *The Film That Changed My Life*, Bogdanovich explains his appreciation of Orson Welles' work.

The 32-year-old Bogdanovich was hailed by critics as a "Wellesian" wunderkind when his best-received film, *The Last Picture Show*, was released in 1971. The film gained eight Academy Awards nominations, including Best Director, and won two statues, for Cloris Leachman and Ben Johnson in the supporting acting categories. Bogdanovich co-wrote the screenplay with Larry McMurtry, and it won the 1971 BAFTA award for Best Screenplay. Bogdanovich cast the 21-year-old model Cybill Shepherd in a major role in the film and fell in love with her, an affair that eventually led to his divorce from Polly Platt, his longtime artistic collaborator and the mother of his two daughters. The affair was referenced, tongue-in-cheek, in an episode of *Moonlighting* where Bogdanovich, being interviewed as himself, claims to have had an affair with Maddie Hayes, Shepherd's character. He was married to Louise Stratten from 1988 to 2001.

Bogdanovich followed up *The Last Picture Show* with the popular comedy *"What's Up, Doc?"* in 1972. starring Barbra Streisand and Ryan O'Neal, a screwball comedy indebted to Hawks's *"Bringing Up Baby"* and *"His Girl Friday"*.[87]

Melvin J. Bagley

A PETER BOGDANOVICH PRODUCTION

MUSIC AND LYRICS BY COLE PORTER

June 30, 1975

Dr. M. J. Bagley
Famous People's Eye
Glasses Museum
61 East Lake Mead Drive
Henderson, Nevada 89015

Dear Dr. Bagley,

    I am happy to add the enclosed pair
of my sunglasses to your collection.

               Best regards,

               Peter Bogdanovich

PB:mw
Enc.

PETER BOGDANOVICH

January 26, 1981

Dr. M. J. Bagley, Director
Famous People's Eye Glasses Museum
61 East Lake Mead Drive
P. O Box 775
Henderson, Nevada 89015

Dear Dr. Bagley:

Enclosed you will find
a pair of Mr. Bogdanovich's
glasses which he wore during
the making of "What's Up Doc?"

As you can see, one of
the lenses needs to be fitted
into the frames and I'm sure
this can be done.

I hope this is what you
are looking for at the Museum.

Sincerely,

Linda Ewen
(Assistant to
 Mr. Bogdanovich)

GUSSIE BUSCH

Born:	August Anheuser Busch II
	March 28, 1899
	St Louis, Missouri, USA
Died:	September 29, 1989 (aged 90)
	St. Louis, Missouri, US
Occupation:	Brewing Executive
Spouse(s):	Marie Church Busch, Elizabeth Overton Busch, Gertrude Buholzer Busch, *Margaret Rohde*
Children:	Carlota Busch Webster, Lilly Busch Hermann August Anheuser Busch III, Elizabeth Busch Burke, Beatrice Busch von Gontard, Peter W. Busch,
	Trudy Busch Valentine, William K. Busch Andrew D. Busch, Adolphus August Busch
Parents:	August Anheuser Busch Sr.

I never drink a beer that does not remind me of the letter that I received from August A. Busch Jr.

August "Gussie" Anheuser Busch, Jr. was an American brewing magnate who built the Anheuser-Busch Companies into the largest brewery in the world as company chairman from 1946 to 1976, and became a prominent sportsman as owner of the St. Louis Cardinals franchise in Major League Baseball from 1953 until his death.

Busch was a grandson of brewery founder Adolphus Busch and grandfather of former CEO August Busch IV. He succeeded his older brother Adolphus Busch III as President and CEO. He began using the Clydesdale team as a company logo in the 1930s. Such Clydesdales were presented to his father pulling a Budweiser beer wagon to commemorate the end of Prohibition.

As chairman, president or CEO of the Cardinals from the time the club was purchased by the brewery in 1963 until his death, Busch oversaw a team that won six National League championships in 1964, 1967, 1968,1982, 1985, 1987 and three World Series in 1964, 1967 and 1982. In 1984, the Cardinals' board of directors retired the uniform number 85, his age at the time.

Busch died at age 90 in St. Louis.[88]

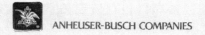

ANHEUSER-BUSCH COMPANIES

August A. Busch, Jr.
Honorary Chairman of the Board

January 28, 1981

Dr. M. J. Bagley, Director
Famous People's Eye Glasses Museum
61 East Lake Mead Drive
Box 775
Henderson, Nevada 89015

Dear Dr. Bagley:

A pair of my old eye glasses is going out
to you today, under separate cover.

I'm delighted to be included in this
illustrious group, and extend my appreciation to you for thinking of me.

With every good wish.

Sincerely,

August A. Busch, Jr.

Anheuser-Busch Companies, Inc.
Executive Offices
721 Pestalozzi Street
St. Louis, MO U.S.A. 63118

BUCKMINSTER FULLER

Born:	July 12, 1895
	Milton, Massachusetts, US
Died:	July 1, 1983 (aged 87)
	Los Angeles, US
Occupation:	Designer, author, inventor
Spouse(s):	Anne Hewlett
Children:	Allegra Fuller Snyder and Alexandra who died in childhood

> The geodesic dome is always a mystery to me on how it is designed and put together, but Buckminster Fuller somehow figured this out.

Richard Buckminster "Bucky" Fuller was an American architect, systems theorist, author, designer, inventor, and futurist.

Fuller published more than 30 books, inventing and popularizing terms such as "Spaceship Earth," ephemeralization, and synergetic. He also developed numerous inventions, mainly architectural designs, including the widely known geodesic dome. Carbon molecules known as fullerenes were later named by scientists for their resemblance to geodesic spheres.

Buckminister Fuller was the second president of Mensa from 1974 to 1983.

Fuller taught at Black Mountain College in North Carolina during the summers of 1948 and 1949 serving as its Summer Institute director in 1949. There, with the support of a group of professors and students, he began reinventing a project that would make him famous: the geodesic dome. Although the geodesic dome had been created some 30 years earlier by Dr. Walther Bauersfeld, Fuller was awarded United States patents. He is credited for popularizing this type of structure.

In 1949, he erected his first geodesic dome building that could sustain its own weight with no practical limits. It was 4.3 meters (14) in diameter and constructed of aluminum aircraft tubing and a vinyl-plastic skin, in the form of an icosahedron. To prove his design, and to awe non-believers, Fuller suspended from the structure's framework several students who had helped him build it. The U.S. government recognized the importance of his work, and employed his firm Geodesics, Inc. in Raleigh, North Carolina to make small domes for the Marines. Within a few years there were thousands of these domes around the world.

Fuller died on July 1, 1983, 11 days before his 88th birthday. During the period leading up to his death, his wife of 66 years had been lying comatose in a Los Angeles Hospital, dying of cancer. It was while visiting her there that he exclaimed, at a certain point: "She is squeezing my hand!" He then stood up, suffered a heart attack, and died an hour later, at age 87. His wife died 36 hours later. They were buried in Mount Auburn Cemetery in Cambridge, Massachusetts.[89]

R. BUCKMINSTER FULLER   3500 Market Street, Philadelphia, Pa. 19104, USA   (215) EV 7-2255   CABLE: "BUCKY"

o **University Professor**
  Southern Illinois University

o **World Fellow in Residence**
  University of Pennsylvania
  Bryn Mawr College
  Haverford College
  Swarthmore College
  University City Science Center

February 18, 1975

Dear Dr. Bagley:

    Dr. Fuller has read your letter of January 8 and asked that I write on his behalf.

    We are presently in search of one of Dr. Fuller's old pairs of eye glasses. As soon as we find one, we shall send it on to you.

              Sincerely,

              Shirley Swansen

              (Miss) Shirley Swansen, CPS
              Administrative Assistant

Dr. M. J. Bagley
Famous People's Eye Museum
61 East Lake Mead Drive
Henderson, Nevada 89015

R. BUCKMINSTER FULLER ● 3500 Market Street, Philadelphia, Pa. 19104 ● USA ● (215) 387–5400 ● CABLE: "BUCKY"

● University Professor Emeritus
  Southern Illinois University
  University of Pennsylvania

● World Fellow in Residence
  University City Science Center

January 30, 1981

Dear Dr. Bagley,

The enclosed pair of eyeglasses are mine, to be added to
the Famous People's Eye Glasses Museum as you requested.

Faithfully,

Buckminster Fuller

Dr. M.J. Bagley
61 East Lake Mead Drive
Henderson, NV 89015

BF/aem

● **Architectural Societies**
  Royal Institute of British Architects, Honorary Fellow
  Royal Architectural Institute of Canada, Honorary Fellow
  American Institute of Architects, Fellow
  Mexican College and Institute of Architects, Member

Society of Venezuelan Architects, Honorary Member
Israel Institute of Engineers and Architects, Honorary Member
Zentralvereinigung Der Architekten Österreichs (Austria), Honorary Member
Association of Siamese Architects Under Royal Patronage, Honorary Member

WILLIAM BALL

Birth name:	William Gormaly Ball
Born:	28 April 1931
	Chicago, Illinois US
Died:	30 July 1991 (aged 60)
	Los Angeles, California US
Occupation:	Theatre director
Awards:	Drama Desk Awards
	Outstanding Director 1959 Ivanov

Most people are not too bashful about their accomplishments, because people already know what made them famous. When I received this letter I had a feeling he was proud about his two famous accomplishments. Never the the less, I am glad to be the new owner of the magical glasses.

William Gormaly Ball was an American stage director and founder of the American Conservatory Theatre (ACT). He was awarded the Drama Desk Vernon Rice Award in 1959 for his production of Chekhov's Ivanov and was nominated for a Tony Award in 1965 for his production of *Moliere's Tartuffe*, starring Michael O'Sullivan and Rene Auberjonois. He was also a noted director of opera.

From 1953 through 1955, he studied acting, design, and directing at Carnegie Mellon University. Ball founded the American Conservatory Theatre in Pittsburgh in 1965. This was a company of up to 30 full-time paid actors who studied all disciplines of the theatre arts during the day and performed at night. Ball had a falling out with ACT's financial benefactors in Pittsburgh and took the company on the road.

In its first season, Ball's ACT produced twenty-seven full length plays in two theaters over the course of seven months. Ball's 1972 production of *Cyrano de Bergerac* and his 1976 production of *"The Taming of the Shrew"* were televised nationally on PBS. In 1979, ACT received the Tony Award for excellence in regional theatre.

Ball was often provocative. His interpretation of Albee's *Tiny Alice* brought threat of a lawsuit from the playwright, who tried to withhold the performance rights only to discover that they had never been granted in the first place. Some observers thought that Ball's operatic production, with an added aside condemning the Vietnam War, may have solved some problems inherent in the text.

Ball was the author of the book, *A Sense of Direction: Some Observations on the Art of Directing*.

Awards he received were Drama Desk Awards, and Outstanding Director 1959 Ivanov.

Ball committed suicide in Los Angeles, California.[90]

WILLIAM BALL

February 3, 1981

Dear Famous People's Eyeglasses Museum:

These glasses are magic because I wore them in the rehearsal periods of two of my finest productions, Taming of the Shrew and Cyrano de Bergerac.

Congratulations on your very innovative collection.

Sincerely,

Bill Ball

STANLEY DANCER

Birth name:	Stanley Franklin Dancer
Born:	July 25, 1927
Died:	September 9, 2005
	Pompano Beach, Florida
Genre:	Horse racer
Nationality:	American

When I was in school in Southern California in the early 50's, my father in law would come to town and we would go to the baggie races. Stanley Dancer Stables was a winner several times and was fascinating to see.

Stanley Franklin Dancer was an American harness racing driver and trainer. He was the only horsemen to drive and train three Triple Crowns in horse racing. In total, he drove 23 Triple Crown winners. He was the first trainer to campaign a horse to $1 million in a career, Cardigan Bay in 1968 and drove the Harness Horse of the Year seven times. During his career, he won over $28 million and 3,781 races and was called by the United States Trotting Association "perhaps the best-known personality in the sport."

Dancer was born in West Windsor Township, New Jersey on July 25, 1927 and grew up on a farm in New

Egypt, New Jersey, living in the area for almost his entire life on a 160-acre farm with a half-mile training track before moving to Pompano Beach, Florida in 1999. He dropped out of school after eighth grade.

He borrowed silks for his first race, driving a horse he had bought for $75, using money he had won from a 4-H Club. He started driving horses at Freehold Raceway in 1945, winning his first race the following year. Dancer started his stable in 1948 with a trotter he had bought using $250 of his wife's college savings. That horse, Candor, took home $12,000 during the following three years.

Dancer died at age 78, in his home in Pompano Beach, Florida from prostate cancer. He was survived by his wife Jody Dancer, whom he married in 1985. He had two sons, two daughters, seven grandchildren and four great-grandchildren. His first marriage, to Rachel Young in 1947, ended in divorce in 1983.

Melvin J. Bagley

STANLEY DANCER STABLES
"EGYPTIAN ACRES" • NEW EGYPT, NEW JERSEY 08533

609-758-8488

February 3, 1981

Famous People's Eye Glasses Museum
61 East Lake Mead Drive
P. O. Box 775
Henderson, Nevada 89015

Attention: Dr. M. J. Bagley
            Director

Dear Dr. Bagley:

     I am sending you, under separate cover, a pair of
my driving glasses of which I used while training and driving
standardbred horses.

                      Sincerely,

                      Stanley Dancer

SD:bwp

274

JEAN STAPLETON

Birth name:	Jeanne Murray
Born:	January 19, 1923
	New York City, New York, US
Died:	May 31, 2013 aged 90
	New York City, New York, US
Cause of death:	Natural causes
Occupation:	Actress
Years active:	1941–2001
Spouse:	William H Putch
Children:	John Putch and Pamela Putch

> She is well known for her character as Edith Bunker on the show *All in the Family*. She has carried the show as well as Caroll O' Connor. Brilliant, in her own right.

Jean Stapleton was born Jeanne Murray on January 19, 1923 and died May 31, 2013, was an American character actress of stage, television and film.

She is best known for her portrayal of Edith Bunker, the long-suffering, yet devoted wife of Archie Bunker, played by Carroll O'Connor, and mother of Gloria Stivic, played by Sally Struthers, on the 1970s situation comedy *All in the Family* Stapleton was also seen occasionally on the *All in the Family* follow-up series, *Archie Bunker's*

Place, but, tired of the role, asked to be written out after the first season.

The daughter of Joseph E. Murray, a billboard advertising salesman, and Marie Stapleton Murray, a singer. At age 18, she began her career in summer stock and made her New York debut in *American Gothic,* an Off-Broadway play.

She received awards for *"All in the Family"* which included three Emmys and two Golden Globes.

Stapleton also appeared in the 1998 feature *You've Got Mail* as a close co-worker in whom Meg Ryan's character confides. Stapleton appeared on the CBS television series *Touched by an Angel* as an angel named Emma.

For 30 years, Stapleton's husband William Putch from 1924 to 1983, directed a summer stock theater, Totem Pole Playhouse, at Caledonia State Park in Fayetteville, Pennsylvania. Stapleton performed regularly at the theatre with the resident company. Together they had two children: director John Putch and television producer Pamela Putch.

Stapleton died, surrounded by family and friends, of natural causes. She was 90.[92]

JEAN STAPLETON

February 8, 1981

Dr. M. J. Bagley, Director
Famous People's Eye Glasses Museum
61 East Lake Mead Drive
Box 775
Henderson, Nevada 89015

Dear Dr. Bagley:

Thank you for your letter inviting
me to send a pair of eyeglasses to
your Museum. Enclosed is a pair
made in '50's style which I wore
on the baseball field in the film,
"Aunt Mary", aired in December 1979
as a Hallmark Hall of Fame Production
on CBS.

Cordially,

Jean Stapleton

PIERRE ANDREW RINFRET

Birth name: Pierre Andre "Pete" Rinfret
Born: February 1, 1924
                Montreal, Canada
Died: June 29, 2006

Receiving glasses from Pierre Rinfret, who served as an economic adviser to three United States Presidents, made a great addition to my collection.

Pierre Andre "Pete" Rinfret was the founder of Rinfret-Boston Associates, an economic advisor to three American Presidents Presidents: John F. Kennedy, Lyndon Johnson, and Richard Nixon. He was the Republican Candidate for Governor of New York in 1990.

His father and the entire family emigrated to the United States from Canada on November 12, 1929.

"We emigrated here because my father had gone bankrupt in his fur business. In Canada that was the ultimate disgrace and he was forced out, socially. He did not know a depression was coming in the U.S. and no one else did either. And so he thought he would have a new start. Little did he know what was ahead. He and all of us had gone from the frying pan into the fire!"

A self-made man, he studied electrical engineering at the University of Maine, and was then drafted into the Army in 1944, where he served General George S. Patton in France and received the Bronze Star. Upon his return he received a MBA from New York University, and spent two years in France as a Fulbright Scholar.

Working in the finance industry, he rose to become chairman of Lionel O. Edie in 1965 before forming his own firm. In 1972, he was a Nixon campaign spokesman, and Nixon offered him a position on the Council of Economic Advisers and later considered him for a cabinet post.

He considered himself a professional financial analyst, first and foremost.

He qualified as a pilot in 2000, at age 76, and died in 2006 at age 82.

He had posted his recollections and impressions of people he had known from politics and business on a web site during his retirement, and carried on a significant online correspondence with people from over twenty countries until just a few months before this death. He was attempting to create an 'online memoir' of his life and experiences, from growing up in the Great Depression, to working with economists such as Milton Friedman and Alan Greenspan.[93]

RINFRET ASSOCIATES, INC.

February 12, 1981

Dr. M. J. Bagley, Director
Famous People's Eye Glasses Museum
61 East Lake Mead Drive
Box 7/5
Henderson, Nevada   89015

Dear Dr. Bagley:

Here is a pair of old, beat-up, helmed eye glasses.

Your idea is a great one!

Most sincerely yours,

Pierre A. Rinfret
President

PAR:JM
ENC

RINFRET ASSOCIATES, INC.
841 Lexington Avenue, N.Y., N.Y. 10022
Telephone: 212-688-2820
Telex: 238171 Seree Ur
Cable Address: Forecast New York

Economic and Financial
Correspondents:
Frankfurt · Hong Kong · Johannesburg
London · Manila · Montreal
Tokyo · Toronto

RINFRET ASSOCIATES FR
11 bis Blvd. Haus
75 Paris, IXe, F
Telephone: Paris 770
Telex: 842 8

THOMAS HINMAN MOORER

Born: February 9, 1912
                    Mount Willing, Alabama, US
Died: February 5, 2004 (aged 91)
                    Bethesda, Maryland, US
Buried at: Arlington National Cemetery
Allegiance: United States of America
Service/branch: United States Navy
Years in Service: 1933-1974
Rank: Admiral
Commands held: Chief of Naval Operations
                    Chairman of the Joint Chiefs of Staff
Battles/wars: World War II, Vietnam War
Awards: Defense Distinguished Service Medal (2)
                    Navy Distinguished Service Medal (5)
                    Silver Star, Legion of Merit
                    Distinguished Flying Cross, Purple Heart
                    Gray Eagle Award

> Ever since my duty in the U.S. Naval Air
> Corps, I have great admiration for any of the
> Naval heroes like Thomas Moorer.

Thomas Hinman Moorer was an Admiral and Naval
Aviator in the United States Navy who served as Chief

of Naval Operations from 1967 to 1970, and as the Chairman of the Joint Chiefs of Staff from 1970 to 1974.

Moorer graduated from the United States Naval Academy on June 1, 1933 and was commissioned an ensign. After completing Naval Aviation training at the Pensacola Naval Air Station in 1936, he flew with fighter squadrons based on the aircraft carriers USS Langley, USS Lexington and USS Enterprise.

In addition to his fighter experience, Moorer also qualified in seaplanes and flew with a patrol squadron in the early years of World War II. Serving with Patrol Squadron Twenty-Two at Pearl Harbor, Hawaii, when the Japanese Empire attacked on December 7, 1941, his squadron subsequently participated in the 1941–1942 Dutch East Awards Indies Campaign in the southwest Pacific, where he flew numerous combat missions. Moorer personally master mined the 1972 mining of Hai Phong Harbor and believed that such an operation, if such an operation had been conducted in 1964, it would have "made a significant difference in the outcome of the war."

Moorer believed that the attack on the USS Liberty in 1967 was a deliberate act on the part of the Israelis and that President Lyndon B. Johnson ordered the cover-up to maintain ties with Israel.[94]

25 February 1981

Dear Dr. Bagley,

I am pleased to send you a pair of my old glasses.
Note that they have been "chewed" on quite a bit.
This due to the fact that they were worn during the
very difficult times of the Vietnam War when I was
serving as Chairman of the Joint Chiefs of Staff.

I am sure these glasses never expected to find them-
selves resting in peace among such famous company.

Best wishes for the future.

Sincerely,

Tom Moorer

Thomas H. Moorer
Admiral, U.S. Navy (Ret)
6901 Lupine Lane
McLean, Va. 22101

Melvin J. Bagley

6 January 1984

Dr. M.J. Bagley
Director
Famous People's Eye Glasses Museum
61 East Lake Mead Drive
Box 775
Henderson, Nevada 89015

Dear Dr. Bagley:

   Your letter of February 15, 1981 addressed to me in
Eufaula, Alabama, reached me a few weeks ago. Enclosed
you will find a pair of eye glasses of mine which, I hope,
you will be able to use for your museum.

                          Sincerely,

                          Thomas H. Moorer

                          Thomas H. Moorer
                          Admiral, U.S. Navy (Ret.)

Enclosure

GILES GORDON

Birth name:	Giles Alexander Esme' Gordon
Born:	23 May 1940
	Edinburgh, Scotland
Died:	November 14, 2003 (aged 63)
	Edinburgh, Scotland

> I guess I should have rewritten Giles Gordon and apologized about not knowing the difference in spectacle and eyeglasses. Never the less, I had to include him in my book since he had written a very interesting letter to me.

Giles Alexander Esmé Gordon was a Scottish literary agent and writer, based for most of his career in London.

The son of an architect, Alexander Gordon and his wife Betsy. Gordon was educated at the Edinburgh Academy, an independent day school. Here he acted in school productions including *Iolanthe*, with future broadcaster Gordon Honeycombe.

In 1966 he released a collection of poems, *Two & Two Make One*, which was published by Akros on a print run of 350 copies. He also wrote half a dozen novels between 1971 and 1980, and later a memoir *"Aren't We Due"* a Royalty Statement in 1993, a title which caused accusations of impropriety by quoting a comment from one of his clients, the Prince of Whales.

He married Margaret Eastoe in 1964; they had two sons and daughter. His daughter Hattie had, at the time of father's death, just published a memoir of her brother Gareth, who had committed suicide in 1994 at the age of 24. His wife Margaret died of an incurable illness in 1989. Gordon's second marriage was to Maggie McKeman in 1990, with whom he had a son and two daughters. Giles Gordon died from injuries sustained in a fall a fortnight earlier outside his home in Edinburgh.[95]

9 St Ann's Gardens, London NW5 4BR, U.K.

27 February 1981

Dr M J Bagley
Director
Famous People's Eye Glasses Museum
61 East Lake Mead Drive
Box 775
Henderson
Nevada 89015

Dear Dr Bagley

I don't know, obviously, to what extent
individuals offer you their eye glasses (or, as we
in the United Kingdom call them, spectacles) as
opposed to your soliciting them.

Nevertheless, I hope you won't think it untoward
of me to offer the Famous People's Eye Glasses
Museum a pair of my old spectacles. They're not
that old, in that I was using them only three or
four years ago.

Were there a Museum such as yours in this country
I'd have offered my old spectacles to it but as
there isn't (and as our Mrs Thatcher and your
Mr Reagan seem to have so much in common) I thought
I'd see what you felt about my spectacles before
doing anything else with them.

Incidentally, and I'm sure you're aware of this,
in our country the term "eye glass" is almost
synonymous with "telescope" or "spy glass", such
as that which Admiral Nelson used at the Battle
of Trafalgar.

I shall look forward to hearing from you.

Yours sincerely

Giles Gordon

MICHAEL TIPPETT

Birth name: Michael Kemp Tippett
Born: 2 January 1905
Died: 8 January 1998

> It surprises me that so many great in their field
> do not receive the fame that I think they deseve.
> This is the case of Sir Michael Tippett.

Sir Michael Kemp Tippett was an English composer.

In his long career he produced a large body of work, including five operas, three large-scale choral works, four symphonies, five string quartets, four piano sonatas, concertos and concertante works, song cycles and incidental music. The works for which he is best known are the *Concerto for Double String Orchestra,* the oratorio *A Child of Our Time* and the *Fantasia Concertante on a Theme of Corelli.*

His deeply held humanitarian and pacifist beliefs shaped both his life and his music. He served a prison sentence as a conscientious objector in the Second World War. An interest in many aspects of contemporary culture is reflected in his music and writings. Tippett was one of the first openly gay composers to explore issues of sexuality in his work. The libretti of his operas, which he wrote himself attracted criticism for their allusion-heavy complexity, and sometimes awkward and not quite idiomatic use of contemporary slang, but have also received praise from, amongst others, noted music critic Andrew Porter, the director Peter Hall and conductor Cohn Davis. Tippett had a keen interest in musical education and in later life was active as a broadcaster and lecturer. As a conductor he recorded many of his own works, as well as making an early recording of Thomas Tallis' 40-part motet *Spem in Alium*. He is generally acknowledged to be one of the most important British composers of the 20th century.[96]

from SIR MICHAEL TIPPETT

Publisher: Schott & Co. Ltd. 48 Great Marlborough Street, London, W1V 2BN Tel. (01) 437-1246/7/8
B. Schott's Söhne   Weihergarten 5   6500 Mainz   Germany.   Tel. 010 49 6131 24341
Agents: Ingpen & Williams.   14 Kensington Court, London W8 5DN.   Tel. (01) 937-5158
Herbert Barrett Management.   1860 Broadway, New York, N.Y. 10023   Tel. 010 1 212 245 3530

```
 DR. M.J. Bagley,                              48 Great Marlborough Street,
Director,                                      London W1
Famous People's Eye Glasses Museum,
61  East Lake Mead Drive,
Box 775,                                       01-439-2640
Henderson,
Nevada 89015
USA
                                               5 March 1981
```

Dear Dr Bagley,

    Sir Michael has asked me to write thanking you for your letter of 15 January, and to let you know that he will shortly be sending you a pair of spectacles for your collection.

With best wishes,

Yours sincerely,

Christopher Senior
Promotional Representative

from SIR MICHAEL TIPPETT

Publisher: Schott & Co. Ltd. 48 Great Marlborough Street, London, W1V 2BN Tel. (01) 437-1246/7/8
B. Schott's Söhne   Weihergarten 5   6500 Mainz   Germany.   Tel. 010 49 6131 24341
Agents: Ingpen & Williams.   14 Kensington Court, London W8 5DN.   Tel. (01) 937-5158
Herbert Barrett Management.   1860 Broadway, New York, N.Y. 10023   Tel. 010 1 212 245 3530

Dr. M.J. Bagley,   48 Great Marlborough Street,
Director,   London W1
Famous Peoples' Eye Glasses Museum,
61 East Lake Mead Drive,
Box 775,   01-439-2640
Henderson,
Nevada 89015   22 April 1981

Dear Dr Bagley,

Further to my letter of 5 March I have pleasure to inform you that
a pair of Sir Michael's Spectacles are on their way to you under
separate cover.

With all good wishes,

Yours sincerely,

Christopher Senior.

Christopher Senior
Promotional Rpereresentative

PS I would be very interested to know of the other exhibits in
your museum.

WILLIAM RUCKELSHAUS

Birth name: William Doyle Ruckelshaus
Born: July 24,1932
                 Indianapolis, Indiana, U.S.
Political party: Republican
Profession: Lawyer

> The name William Ruckelshaus has always intrigued me because usually or sometimes you can mistake two people with the same name. In this case, I have never, before or after, heard the name Ruckelshaus.

William Doyle Ruckelshaus is an American attorney and former U.S. government official. He served as the first head of the Environmental Protection Agency (EPA) in 1970, was subsequently acting Director of the Federal Bureau of Investigation, and then Deputy Attorney General of the United States. in 1983 he was the 5th Administrator of the Environmental Protection Agency.

In 1983, with the EPA in crisis due to mass resignations over the mishandling of the Superfund project, President Ronald Reagan appointed Ruckelshaus to serve as EPA Administrator again. This time it was White House Chief of Staff James Baker who was Ruckelshaus's champion in asking him to return to the agency. The White House acceded to Ruckelshaus's request to allow him maximum autonomy in the choice of new appointees.

Ruckelshaus attempted to win back public confidence in the EPA, a challenging task in the face of a skeptical press and a wary Congress both of whom scrutinized all aspects of the agency's activities and some of whom interpreted a number of its actions in the worst possible light. Nonetheless, Ruckelshaus filled the top-level staffing slots with persons of competence, turned the attention of the staff back to the agency's fundamental mission, and raised the esteem of the agency in the public mind.

"I've had an awful lot of jobs in my lifetime, and in moving from one to another, have had the opportunity to think wait what makes them worthwhile. I've concluded there are four important criteria: interest, excitement, challenge, and fulfillment. I've never worked anywhere where I could find all four to quite the same extent as at EPA. I can find interest challenge and excitement. I do have an interesting job. But it is tough to find the same degree of fulfillment I found in the government. At EPA, you work for a cause that is beyond self-interest and larger than the goals people normally pursue. You're not there for the money, you're there for something beyond yourself."[97]

Weyerhaeuser Company

William D. Ruckelshaus
Senior Vice President

Tacoma, Washington 98401
(206) 924-2219

March 4, 1981

Dr. M. J. Bagley, Director
Famous People's Eye Glasses Museum
61 East Lake Mead Drive
Box 775
Henderson NV 89015

Dear Dr. Bagley:

Per your request of February 15, enclosed please find
a pair of Mr. Ruckelshaus' old eye glasses which he
requested I contribute to your museum.

Sincerely yours,

Diane Roline
for W. D. Ruckelshaus

DR:dh30/325/c4

Enclosure

GUS HALL

General Secretary of the National Committee of the Communist Party USA

Birth name:	Arvo Kustaa Halberg
Born:	October 8, 1910
	Cherry Township,
	Minnesota, United States
Died:	October 13, 2000
	Lenox Hill Hospital
	Manhattan, New York.
	United States
Political party:	Communist Party USA
Spouse(s):	Elizabeth Mary Turner
Children:	Arvo, Barbara
Residence:	Yonkers, New York
Alma mater:	International Lenin School
Occupation:	Lumberjack, miner, steel worker, trade unionist, political writer

Diversification seems to be the trademark of the things that make this book unique. Even in this case, where we have no idea of their political affiliation, then his guy came along.

Gus Hall was born Arvo Kustaa Halberg and was a leader and Chairman of the Communist Party USA (CPUSA) and its four-time US presidential candidate. As a labor leader, Hall was closely associated with the so-called "Little Steel" Strike of 1937, an effort to unionize the nation's smaller, regional steel manufacturers. During the Second Red Scare, Hall was indicted under the Smith Act and was sentenced to eight years in prison. After his release, Hall led the CPUSA for over 40 years, often taking an orthodox Marxist-Leninist stance.

At 15, to support the impoverished ten-child family, Hall left school and went to work in the North Woods lumber camps, mines and railroads. Two years later in 1927, he was recruited to the CPUSA by his father.

In Youngstown, Hall met Elizabeth Mary Turner, a woman of Hungarian background. They were married in 1935. Hall's wife for 65 years, Elizabeth was a leader in her own right, among the first women steelworkers and a secretary of SWOC. They had two children, Barbara and Arvo.[98]

GUS HALL

March 10, 1981

Dr. M.J. Bagley
Director
Famous People's Eye Glasses Museum
61 East Lake Mead Drive
Box 775
Henderson, Nevada 89015

Dear Dr. Bagley,

I was delighted to receive your request dated January 15th, and am pleased to send you under separate cover an old pair of my eye glasses. I certify that these glasses are authentic.

I am indeed honored that your museum desires to exhibit the eye glasses of the General Secretary of the Communist Party, U.S.A., a person who sees all things from a socialist perspective, one who's vision of our country's future encompasses all those who see the need for peace, detente, socialism and a struggle against racism and all forms of inequality.

Again, my sincere appreciation for choosing to solicit my eye glasses for your museum and for considering the outlook of a Communist Party USA member worthy of your Famous People's Eye Glasses Museum.

Best of luck and success in your endeavor.

Sincerely,

Gus Hall

GH/cam

FRED ROGERS

Birth name:	Fred McFeely Rogers
Born:	March 20, 1928
	Latrobe, Pennsylvania
Died:	February 27, 2003 (aged 74)
	Pittsburgh, Pennsylvania
Cause of Death:	Stomach cancer
Occupation:	Educator, minister, songwriter television host.
Years Active:	1951-2001
Religion:	Presbyterian Church (USA)
Spouse(s):	Sara Joanne Byrd

> In the early 90's, my secretary was a babysitter
> and was only allowed to watch TV two hours a
> day. She told me that *Mr. Roger's Neighborhood*
> was one of the kid's favorite programs.

Fred McFeely Rogers was an American educator,
Presbyterian minister, songwriter, author, and television
host. Rogers was most famous for creating and hosting
Mister Rogers Neighborhood from 1968 to 2001, which
featured his gentle, soft-spoken personality and direct-
ness to his audiences.

Initially educated to be a minister, Rogers was displeased with the way television addressed children and
made an effort to change this when he began to write for

and perform on local Pittsburgh-area shows dedicated to youth. Over the course of three decades on television, Fred Rogers became an indelible American icon of children's entertainment and education, as well as a symbol of compassion, patience, and morality. He was also known for his advocacy of various public causes.

Rogers received the Presidential Medal of Freedom, some forty honorary degrees, and a Peabody Award. He was inducted into the Television Hall of Fame, was recognized by two Congressional resolutions, and was ranked No. 35 among TV Guide's Fifty Greatest TV Stars of All Time. Several buildings and artworks in Pennsylvania are dedicated to his memory, and the Smithsonian Institution displays one of his trademark sweaters as a "Treasure of American History."

At College, in Winter Park, Florida, he met Sara Joanne Byrd, an Oakland, Florida native; they married on June 9, 1952. They had two sons, James and John. In 1963 Rogers graduated from Pittsburgh Theological Seminary and was ordained a minister in the Presbyterian Church.

Rogers had an apartment in New York City and a summer home on Nantucket island in Massachusetts. Rogers was red-green color blind, swam every morning, was a vegetarian, and neither smoked nor drank. Despite recurring rumors, he never served in the military.

Roger died of stomach cancer.[99]

Family Communications Inc.
4802 Fifth Avenue
Pittsburgh, Pennsylvania 15213
412/687-2990

March 11, 1981

Dr. M. J. Bagley
Famous People's Eye Glasses Museum
61 East Lake Mead Drive
Box 775
Henderson, Nevada   89015

Dear Dr. Bagley,

These glasses helped me write many MISTER ROGERS' NEIGHBORHOOD
scripts.

Sincerely,

Fred Rogers

FR/sn

enclosure

RICHARD M. SCAMMON

Birth name:	Richard M. Scammon
Born:	1915–2001
Nationality:	American
Occupation:	American Author, Political Scientist, Election Scholar

> In the 70's I watched his election news on NBC. Richard Scammon was on, working the election results.

Richard M. Scammon was born in Minnesota in 1915. He was an American author, political scientist and election's scholar. He served as Director of the U.S. Bureau of the Census from 1961 to 1965. Afterwards, he worked for decades directing election analysis for NBC News.

Scammon was born in Minnesota, and earned a bachelor's degree in Political Science from the University of Minnesota in 1935. He later earned a master's degree from the University of Michigan, also in political science.

Scammon enlisted in the Army during World War II, attaining the rank of Captain. He served in occupied Germany after the war, rising to head the military government's office of elections and political parties. After his discharge, he served as chief of the research division in Western Europe for the U.S. Department of State from 1948 to 1955.

Scammon founded the Elections Research Center in 1955 after leaving government service. Its enduring contribution was the long-running series of volumes, *America Votes,* which for the first time provided standard and reliable statistics for the results of major elections in all 50 states.

In 1961, President John F. Kennedy appointed Scammon as Census Director, which he continued until 1965, during the administration of Lyndon B. Johnson. According to the *Washington Post,* while serving as Director of the Census, Scammon was "a personal adviser to Presidents Kennedy and Johnson on public opinion and political trends."

Returning to his voting research, Scammon was hired by NBC News to direct its extensive election-night coverage in November 1968. He continued his work as a consultant for NBC until 1988.

As an author, Scammon's most famous work was *The Real Majority: An Extraordinary Examination of the American Electorate* in 1970, co-authored with Bend, Wattenberg.

Scammon was married to Mary Allen Scammon and lived in Chevy Chase, Maryland for five decades. He died of Alzheimer's disease at a rest home in Gaithersburg.[100]

Melvin J. Bagley

ELECTIONS RESEARCH CENTER
1619 MASSACHUSETTS AVENUE, N.W.
WASHINGTON, D. C. 20036

202-387-6066

March 18, 1981

Dr. M. J. Bagley, Director
Famous People's Eye Glasses Museum
61 East Lake Mead Drive
Box 775
Henderson, Nevada 89015

Dear Dr. Bagley,

      Please find enclosed a pair of eyeglasses which
I wore back in the 1970's--including election night in November 1972
at N.B.C. in New York where I was serving as an elections consultant
to the network.

Sincerely,

Richard M. Scammon
Director

Editors and Compilers of "AMERICA VOTES"

ERICA JONG

Birth name:	Erica Mann
Born:	March 26, 1942
	New York City, United States
Pen name:	Erica Jong
Occupation:	Author and teacher
Nationality:	American
Period:	1973-present
Genres:	Primarily fiction and poetry
Notable:	Fear of Flying, *Shylock's*
work(s):	*Daughter Seducing the Demon*
Spouse(s):	Michael Werthman, Allan Jong, Jonathan Fast, Kenneth David Burrows
Children:	Molly Jong-Fast

Erica Jong is an American author and teacher best known for her fiction and poetry.

A 1963 graduate of Barnard College with an MA in 1965 in 18th century English Literature from Columbia University, Erica Jong is best known for her first novel, *Fear of Flying* in 1973, which created a sensation with its frank treatment of a woman's sexual desires. Although it contains many sexual elements, the book is mainly the account of a hypersensitive young woman, in her late twenties, trying to find who she is and where she is going.

It contains many psychological, humorous, descriptive elements, and rich cultural and literary references. The book tries to answer the many conflicts arising in women in late1960s and early 1970s America, of womanhood, femininity, love, one's quest for freedom and purpose.

Jong has been married four times. Her first two marriages, to college sweetheart Michael Werthman, and to Allan Jong, a Chinese American psychiatrist, reflect those of the narrator of *Fear of Flying*. Her third husband was Jonathan Fast, a novelist and social work educator, and son of novelist Howard Fast. This marriage was described in *How to Save Your Own Life* and *Parachutes and Kisses*. She has a daughter from her third marriage, Molly Jong-Fast. Jong is now married to Kenneth David Burrows, a New York litigation attorney. In the late 1990s, Jong wrote an article about her current marriage in the magazine *Talk*.

Jong lived for three years, 1966 to 1969, in Heidelberg, Germany, with her second husband, on an army base. She was a frequent visitor to Venice, and wrote about that city in her novel, *Shylock's Daughter*. Jong is mentioned in the Bob Dylan song "Highlands."

Jong supports LGBT rights and legalization of same-sex marriage and she claims that "Gay marriage is a blessing not a curse. It certainly promotes stability and family. And its certainly good for kids."[101]

ERICA JONG

Dr. M. J. Bagley
Director
Famous People's Eye Glasses Museum
61 East Lake Mead Drive
Henderson, Nevada 89015

Dear Dr. Bagley,

These are the glasses through
which I wrote HOW TO SAVE YOUR OWN
LIFE. Since I am retiring them
from active service, I thought you
would like to have them for the
Museum.

Sincerely,

April 17, 1981

MILOS FORMAN

Birth name:	Jan Tomas Forman
Born:	February 18, 1932
	Caslav, Czechoslovakia
Occupation:	Actor, Director, Screenwriter
Years active:	1953-present
Spouse(s):	Jana Brejchova, Vera Kresadlova-Formanova, Martina Zborilova-Forman

One flew over the Cuchoo's Nest was most often associated with the acting of Jack Nicholson consequently this great story was often over look by this great director Milos Forman.

Jan Tomás Forman is a Czech-American director, screenwriter, and professor, who until 1968 had lived and worked primarily in the former Czechoslovakia.

Forman was one of the most important directors of the Czechoslovak New Wave. His 1967 film *The Fireman's Ball,* on the face of it a naturalistic representation of an ill-fated social event in a provincial town, has been viewed by both movie scholars and the then-authorities in Czechoslovakia as a biting satire on East European Communism, which resulted in its being banned for many years in Forman's home country.

Since Forman left Czechoslovakia, two of his films, *"One Flew Over the Cuckoo's Nest"* and *Amadeus,* have acquired particular renown, both gaining him an Academy Award for Best Director. *"One Flew Over the Cuckoo's Nest"* was the second to win all five major Academy Awards Best Picture, Actor in Lead Role, Actress in Lead Role, Director, and Screenplay following *"It Happened One Night"* in 1934, an accomplishment not repeated until 1991 by *The Silence of the Lambs.* He was also nominated for a Best Director Oscar for The *People vs. Larry Flynt* He has also won Golden Globe, Cannes, Berlinale, BAFTA, Cesar, David di Donatello, European Film Academy, and Czech Lion awards.

Forman's first wife was Czech movie star Jana Brejchova. They married in 1958 and divorced in 1962. He then married his second wife Czech actress Vera Kresadlova-Formanova. Together they have twin sons Petr and Matej and are involved in the theater. They were born in 1964. The second marriage lasted for 34 years from 1964 to 1999. Forman married Martina Zborilova on November 28, 1999. They also have twin sons born in 1999, Jim and Andy, and reside in Connecticut.[102]

Melvin J. Bagley

"RAGTIME"
1619 Broadway
New York City, New York   10019

April 27th, 1981

Dr. M.J. Bagley
Famous People's Eye Glasses Museum
61 East Lake Mead Drive
Box 775
Henderson, Nevada   89015

Dear Dr. Bagley;

    I apologize for the delay in sending Milos Forman's
glasses, but he wanted to be absolutely certain that
his new perscription was indeed an improvement over
these trusty companions.

    Milos wore these glasses during the principle
photography of his current project "RAGTIME".
They were faithful to the end.   I hopethat they
find a comfortable home in the museum.

    Thank you for your unusual request.

                    Sincerely,

                    Amy Ness

                    Amy Ness
                    (For Milos Forman)

ENCLOSURE

PAUL SIMON

Birth name:	Paul Frederic Simon
Born:	October 13, 1941
	Newark, New Jersey, United States
Genres:	Folk rock, folk music, soft rock, worldbeat
Occupations:	Musician, singer-songwriter, record producer, arranger
Instruments:	vocals, guitar, bass guitar, piano, percussion, lute, also saxophone, piccolo.
Years active:	1957 – present
Labels:	Columbia, Warner Bros., Hear Music
Associated Acts:	Simon & Garfunkel

Paul Frederic Simon was born in Newark, New Jersey, and is an American musician, singer and songwriter. Simon's fame, influence, and commercial success began as part of the duo Simon & Garfunkel, formed in 1964 with musical partner Art Garfunkel. Simon wrote most of the pair's songs, including three that reached No. 1 on the US singles chart, "The Sound of Silence," "Mrs. Robinson" and "Bridge Over Troubled Water" The duo split up in 1970 at the height of their popularity, and Simon began a successful solo career as a guitarist and singer-songwriter, recording three highly acclaimed albums over the next five years. In 1986, he released *Graceland,* and album inspired by South African township music. Simon also wrote and starred in the film *One-Trick Pony* in 1980 and co-wrote the Broadway musical *The Capeman* in 1998 and the poet Derek Walcott.

Simon has earned 12 Grammys for his solo and collaborative work, including the Lifetime Achievement Award. In 2001, he was inducted into the Rock and Roll Hall of Fame and in 2006 was selected as one of the "100 People Who Shaped the World" by *Time* magazine.

Among many other honors, Simon was the first recipient of the Library of Congress's Gershwin Prize for Popular Song in 2007. In 1986 Simon was awarded an Honorary Doctor of Music degree from Berklee College of Music where he currently serves on the Board of Trustees.

When Simon moved to England in 1964, he met Kathleen Mary "Kathy" Chitty on April 12, at the first English folk club he played, The Hermit Club in Brentwood, Essex, where Chitty worked part-time selling tickets. She was 17, he was 22, and they fell in love. Later that year they visited the US together, touring around mainly by bus. Kathy returned to England on her own with Simon returning to her some weeks later. When Simon returned to the US with the growing success of "The Sound Of Silence" Kathy, who was quite shy, wanted no part of the success and fame that awaited Simon and they split up.

Simon has been married three times, first to Peggy Harper in 1969. They had a son Harper Simon in 1972 and divorced in 1975. His second wife was Carrie Fisher from 1983 to 1984. His third wife is Edie Brickell on

May 30, 1992. They have three children together; Adrian, Lulu and Gabriel.[103]

PAUL SIMON

36 EAST 61ST STREET, NEW YORK

15 May 1981

Dr. M.J. Bagley
Famous People's Eye Glasses Museum
61 East Lake Mead Drive
Box 775
Henderson, Nevada 89015

Dear Dr. Bagley:

Your letter to Paul Simon of January 15, 1981 has been referred to me for reply.

Paul has asked me to thank you for inviting him to donate a pair of eyeglasses to your museum but unfortunately there is the small problem of his 20/20 vision.

If at some later date this situation should change be assured that I have kept your letter on file and will contact you then.

With best wishes.

Yours sincerely,

IAN E. HOBLYN

DANIEL BELL

Born:	May 10, 1919
	New York City, New York, United States
Died:	January 25 2011 (age 91)
	Cambridge, Massachusetts, United States
Fields:	Sociology
Institutions:	University at Chicago,
	Columbia University, Harvard University
Alma mater:	City College at New York, Columbia University
Known for:	Post-Industrialism

Anybody that ended up as a professor emeritus at Harvard University, has got to be brilliant. This is the case of Daniel Bell.

Daniel Bell was an American sociologist, writer, editor, and professor emeritus at Harvard University, best known for his seminal contributions to the study of post-industrialism. He has been described as "one of the leading American intellectuals of the postwar era." His three best known works are *The End of Ideology* *The Coming of Post-Industrial Society* and the *Cultural Contradictions of Capitalism.*

His parents, Benjamin and Anna Bolotsky, were originally from Eastern Europe. They worked in the garment industry. His father died when he was eight months old, and he grew up poor living with relatives along with his mother and his older brother. At age 13, the family name was changed form Bolotsky to Bell.

Bell graduated form Stuyvesant High School and City College of New York with a Bachelor's Degree in Science and Social Science in 1938, and studied for one year further at Columbia University in 1938 to 1939.

Bell's son, David Bell, is a professor of French history at Princeton University, and his daughter, Jordy Bell, was an Academic Administrator and Teacher of, among other things, U.S. Women's history at Marymount College, Tarrytown, New York, before her retirement in 2005.

Bell lived in Cambridge, Massachusetts, with his wife Pearl Bell, a Scholar of Literary Criticism. He died at home on January 25, 2011.[104]

HARVARD UNIVERSITY

DEPARTMENT OF SOCIOLOGY

DANIEL BELL
Henry Ford II Professor
of Social Sciences

William James Hall 370
Cambridge, Massachusetts 02138
617-495-3843

May 21, 1981

Dr. M. J. Bagley
Famous People's Eye Glasses
  Museum
61 East Lake Mead Drive
Box 775
Henderson, Nevada 89015

Dear Dr. Bagley:

In response to your letter of January 15th, I am sending you a pair of my glasses to add to your museum.

Sincerely,

Daniel Bell

Daniel Bell

DB:am

Enc.

BETTY WHITE

Birth name:	Betty Marion White
Born:	January 17, 1922
	Oak Park, Illinois, US
Other Names:	Gerrie, Betty White Ludden
Education:	Horace Mann School
Alma mater	Beverly Hills High School
Occupation:	Actress, comedienne, writer
Years active:	1939-present
Home Town:	Beverly Hills, California, USA
Television:	*Life with Elizabeth, Date with the Angels*
	The Mary Tyler Moore Show, The Betty White Show
	The Golden Girls, The Golden Palace
	Hot in Cleveland, Betty White's Off Their Rockers
Spouse(s):	Dick Barker, Lane Allen, Allen Ludden

My favorite Goldren Girl and still alive. She must have loved Allen Luden very much to include his glasses with hers in my museum.

Betty Marion White Ludden, better known as Betty White, is an American actress, comedienne, singer, author and television personality. With a career spanning over nine decades, she is known to contemporary audiences for her television roles as Sue Ann Nivens on *The Mary*

Tyler Moore Show and Rose Nylund on *The Golden Girls.* Since the death of co-star Rue McClanahan in 2010, she is the only surviving Golden Girl. She currently stars as Elka Ostrovsky in the TV Land sitcom *Hot in Cleveland* for which she has won two consecutive Screen Actors Guild Awards. She currently hosts the practical-joke show *Betty White's Off Their Rockers.*

Betty White has won a Grammy, as well as six Emmy Awards, receiving 20 Emmy nominations over her career, including being the first woman to receive an Emmy for game show hosting for the short-lived Just Men and is the only person to have an Emmy in all female performing comedic categories. In May 2010, White became the oldest person to guest-host *Saturday Night Live,* for which she received a Primetime Emmy Award. White also holds the record for longest span between Emmy nominations for performances; -her first was in 1951 and her most recent was in 2012, a span of 61 years. She has become the oldest nominee as of 2012, aged 90. She has made regular appearances on the game shows *Password and Match Game* and played recurring roles on *Mama's Family, Boston Legal, The Bold and the Beautiful, That '70s Show,* and *Community.*

White has won six Emmy Awards, three American Comedy Awards, (including a lifetime Achievement Award in 1990), and two Viewer for Quality Television Awards. She was inducted into the television Hall of Fame in 1995 and has a star on the Hollywood Walk of Fame at 6747 Hollywood Boulevard alongside the star of her husband, Allen Ludden.[105]

December 29, 1987

Dr. M. J. Bagley
61 East Lake Mead Dr.
Henderson, NV 89015

Dear Dr. Bagley:

What a wonderful idea! The little gray pair
were mine and the other pair belonged to my
beloved husband, Allen Ludden. Perhaps you
would like to include him in your Museum.

Thanks for thinking of us. Best wishes for
the New Year.

Sincerely,

Betty White

BW/gc
Encls.

DAVID L. WOLPER

Birth name:	David Lloyd Wolper
Born:	January 11, 1928
	York City, New York, United States
Died:	August 10, 2010 (age 82)
	Beverly Hills, California, United States
Occupation:	Producer
Spouse(s):	Toni Carroll, Margaret Dawn Richard, Gloria Diane Hill

I am happy to have glasses from a great film producer of his time.

David Lloyd Wolper was an American television and film producer, responsible for shows such as *Roots*, *The Thorn Birds*, *North & South*, *L.A. Confidential*, and the film *Willy Wonka & the Chocolate Factory*. He also produced numerous documentaries and documentary series like *Biography*, from 1961 to 1963, *The Rise and Fall of the Third Reich*, *Appointment with Destiny* (TV), *This Is Elvis*, *Pour Days in November*, *Imagine: John Lennon*, and others. He directed the 1959 documentary *The Race for Space*, which was nominated for an Academy Award. His 1971 film, (as executive producer,) about the study of insects, *The Hellstmm Chronicle*, won an Academy Award.

Wolper was the son of Anna Fass and Irving S. Wolper. For his work on television, he had received a star on the Hollywood Walk of Fame.

On March 13, 1974, one of his crews, filming a National Geographic history of Australopithecus at Mammoth Mountain Ski Area, was killed when the Corvair 440 Sierra Pacific Airlines plane exploded on takeoff from Eastern Sierra Regional Airport in Bishop, California. The filmed segment was recovered in the wreckage and was broadcast in the television series *Primal Man*. The NTSB never determined the cause of the accident and the resort sold the airline.

Wolper died on August 10, 2010 of congestive heart disease and complications of Parkinson's disease at his Beverly Hills' home. Wolper was survived by his wife of 36 years Gloria Hill, his three children from a previous marriage; sons Mark and Michael Wolper and a daughter Leslie. He was also survived by 10 grandchildren.[106]

DAVID L.WOLPER PRODUCTIONS, INC.

OFFICE OF THE PRESIDENT   April 14, 1988

Dr. M.J. Bagley
Director
Famous People's Eye Glasses Museum
61 East Lake Mead Drive
Box 775
Henderson, Nevada 89015

Dear Dr. Bagley:

Please find enclosed a pair of totoise-frame bifocal
glasses which I attest are my own. I hope they will add
interest to your museum, and thank you for asking me to
participate.

Cordially,

David L. Wolper

enclosure

NORM CROSBY

Birth name:	Norman Lawrence Crosby
Born:	September 15, 1927
	Boston, Massachusetts
Occupation:	Comedian
Spouse(s):	Joan Crane Foley

> Now here is a funny guy with a completely different, like Bob Hope.

Norm Crosby is an American comedian sometimes associated with the Borscht Belt who often appeared on television in the 1970s. He is known for his use of malapropisms and is often called The Master of Malaprop. He was born in Boston.

Crosby went solo as a standup comedian, adopting a friendly, blue collar, guy-next- door attitude in the 1950s. Norm Crosby refined his standup monologues by interpolating malapropisms. In 1968, he co-starred on *The Beautiful Phyllis Diller Show,* an NBC-TV summer series. In 1974, he co-hosted a Canadian variety television series, *Everything Goes.* From 1978 to 1981, Crosby hosted the nationally syndicated series, *The Comedy Shop,* aka *Norm Cosby's Comedy Shop.*

In the late 1970s and early 1980s, Crosby became a commercial pitchman for Anheuser-Busch Natural Light beer.

From 1983 until the program's disassociation with Jerry Lewis, Norm Crosby co-hosted and contributed to the annual Jerry Lewis MDA Labor Day Telethon. He has a star on the Hollywood Walk of Fame at 6560 Hollywood Boulevard, Los Angeles.

Crosby has been a Freemason since 1956, having served as Master of at least one lodge and participated in many charitable activities. As of September 2005, he was a member of Ionic Composite Lodge 520 in Los Angeles, California.

Crosby is a native of Dorchester, Massachusetts, a dissolved municipality and current neighborhood of Boston, Massachusetts.[107]

NORM CROSBY

November 1988

Dr. M.J.Bagley
Director

Dear Dr. Bagley,

Please be insured that these spectaculars were once worn by me to insist me in reading my own material in reparation to becoming a humidor.

Needless to say, they were not very lucid because I write now just the way I talk. However, there is some concilliation in the fact that if I were more deficient in my speech then I would have no career and you wouldn't want my glasses anyway.

With warmest good wishes,

Norm Crosby

LIZ CLAIBORNE
Fashion Designer

Birth name:	Anne Elisabeth Jane Claiborne
Born:	March 31, 1929
	Brussels, Belgium
Nationality:	American
Occupation:	Fashion Designer
Labels:	Liz Claiborne

> As part of my business as an optometrist, we sold a few designer glass frames. Liz Claiborne's name was magic and we sold many of her designer frames in my office.

Anne Elisabeth Jane "Liz" Claiborne was a Belgian-born American fashion designer and entrepreneur. Claiborne is best known for co-founding Liz Claiborne Inc. which in 1986 became the first company founded by a woman to make the Fortune 500. Claiborne was the first woman to become chairperson and CEO of a Fortune 500 Company.

Claiborne was born in Brussels to American parents. She came from a prominent Nationality American Louisiana family with an ancestor William CC. Claiborne having been Governor of Louisiana during the War of 1812. In 1939, at the start of World War II, the family returned to New Orleans. She attended St. Timothy's, a boarding school then in Catonsville, Maryland and currently in Stevenson, Maryland. Rather than finishing high school, she went to Europe to study art in painters' studios. Her father did not believe that she needed an education, so she studied art informally.

In 1949, she won the Jacques Heim National Design Contest, sponsored by Harper's Bazaar, and then moved to New York City where she worked for years in the Garment District on Seventh Avenue as a sketch artist at the sportswear house Tina Leser. She worked as a designer for Dan Keller and Youth Group Inc.

Claiborne had a short-lived marriage before marrying Art Ortenberg in 1957. She had a son from her first marriage and two stepchildren from her second.

On May 1998 she was advised that she had a rare form of cancer affecting the lining of her abdomen. She died at the age of 78, after a nine year battle with cancer.[108]

January 12, 1989

Dear Dr. Bagley:

Thanks for your recent letter inviting me to be a part of your Famous People's Eye Glasses Museum. I am more than happy to participate and I am certainly in very good company!

These are the frames that launched what is now considered to be my signature look! I have to be honest though, since we started an eye glass business, I now wear all different shapes and colors! But, my all-time favorite is the big, round tortoise frames!

Enjoy the frames.

Sincerely,

Liz Claiborne

BROOKS ROBINSON

Born:	May 18, 1937
	Little Rock Arkansas
Batted:	Right
Threw:	Right
MLB debut:	September 17, 1955, for the Baltimore Orioles
MLB Appearance:	August 13, 1977 for the Baltimore Orioles
Career Statistics:	Batting average–267, Hits- 2848, Home runs -268 Runs batted in -1357
Teams:	Baltimore Orioles (1955-1977)

What a clever nickname for a great baseball player, "The Human Vacuum Cleaner." A vacuum picks up everything, as did he.

Brooks Calbert Robinson, Jr. is an American former professional baseball player. He played his entire 23-year major league career for the Baltimore Orioles from 1955 to 1977. He was nicknamed "The Human Vacuum Cleaner." He is generally acclaimed as the greatest defensive third-baseman in major league history. He won 16 consecutive Gold Glove Awards during his career, tied with pitcher Jim Kaat for the second most all-time for any player at any position. Robinson was elected to the Baseball Hall of Fame in 1983.

Robinson was selected for the All-Star team in 15 consecutive years from 1960 to 1974, and played in four World Series. He compiled a .267 career batting average with 2,848 home runs and 1357 runs batted in. Robinson led the American League in fielding percentage a record eleven times, at his retirement, his .971 career fielding average was the highest ever for a third baseman. His totals of 2,870 games played at third base, 2697 career putouts, 6205 career assists, 8902 career total chances and 618 double plays, were records for third baseman at the time of his retirement.

He met his future wife, Constance Louise "Connie" Butcher, on one of the Orioles team flight from Kansas City to Boston in July 1959, where she was a flight attendant for United Air Lines. He was smitten with her that he kept ordering iced tea from her. After drinking his third glass of tea, he returned it to her in the galley. He told her, "I want to tell you something. If any of these guys, the Baltimore Orioles, asked you for a date, tell 'em you don't date married men. Understand? I'm the only single guy on the team." Before the plane landed in Boston the two had made a date. He was not the only single guy in the trip he lied to her to keep her from talking to other guys. Brooks and Constance were married in her hometown of Windsor, Ontario, Canada on October 8, 1960.

On March 31, 2011, Robinson was admitted to Greater Baltimore Medical Center for emergency surgery after he developed an infection and fever. In the two weeks he spent in the hospital, he received an outpouring of letters and well-wishes from fans around the country. He had also previously been successfully treated for prostate cancer in 2009.[109]

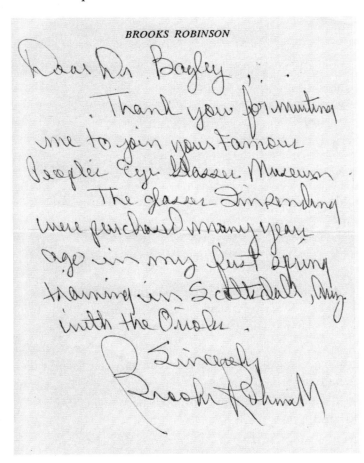

BROOKS ROBINSON

Dear Dr Bagley,

Thank you for inviting me to join your famous People's Eye Glasses Museum. The glasses I'm sending were purchased many years ago in my first spring training in Scottsdale, Ariz, with the Orioles.

Sincerely,
Brooks Robinson

RUDY VALLEE

Birth name:	Hubert Prior Vallee
Born:	July 28, 1901
	Island Pond, Vermont, US
Died:	July 3, 1986 (aged 84)
	North Hollywood, Los Angeles, California, US
Occupations:	Singer, actor, bandleader, entertainer
Instruments:	Saxophone
Years active:	1924-1984
Labels:	RCA Victor

I think he was the first to be called "The Great Crooner", although he had many other talents. He was an outstanding entertainer.

Rudy Vallée was an American singer, actor, bandleader, and entertainer.

Rudy Vallée was born Hubert Prior Vallée in Island Pond, Vermont, the son of Charles Alphonse and Catherine Lynch Vallée. Both of his parents were born and raised in Vermont, but his grandparents were immigrants. The Vallées were French Canadians from neighboring Quebec, while the Lynches were from Ireland. Vallée grew up in Westbrook, Maine.

Vallée became the most prominent and, arguably, the first of a new style of popular singer, the crooner. Previously, popular singers needed strong projecting voices to fill theaters in the days before the electric microphone. Crooners had soft voices that were well suited to the intimacy of the new medium of the radio. Vallée's trombone-like vocal phrasing on *Deep Night* would inspire later crooners such as Bing Crosby, Frank Sinatra, and Perry Como to model their voices on jazz instruments.

In 1929, Vallée made his first feature film, *The Vagabond Lover* for RKO Radio. His first films were made to cash in on his singing popularity. Despite Vallée's rather wooden initial performances, his acting greatly improved in the late 1930s and 940s. Also in 1929, Vallée began hosting *The Fleischmann's Yeast Hour* a very popular radio show at the time.

Vallée continued hosting popular radio variety shows through the 1930s and 1940s. *The Royal Gelatin Hour* featured various film performers of the era, such as Fay Wray and Richard Cromwell in dramatic skits.

Vallee was married briefly to actress Jane Greer, but that ended in divorce in 1944. His previous marriage to Leonie Cauchois was annulled and the one to Fay Webb ended in divorce. After divorcing Jane Greer, he married Eleonor Norris in 1946, who wrote a memoir, *My Vagabound Lover*. Their marriage lasted until his death in 1986.

Vallee died of cancer at his home on July 3, 1986.[110]

rom the desk of

My time___ is your time,___

RUDY VALLÉE

My dear Dr. Bagley:

Enclosed the glasses you asked me to send!!

Cordially,

BARBARA STANWYCK

Birth name:	Ruby Catherine Stevens
Born:	July 16, 1907
	Brooklyn, New York, US
Died:	January 20, 1990 (aged 82)
	Santa Monica, California, US
Cause of Death:	Congestive heart failure and chronic obstructive pulmonary disease
Occupation:	Actress
Years Active:	1922-1986
Spouse(s)	Frank Fay (1928-1935) Robert Taylor (1939-1951)
Children:	1

When I got these glasses, they were sent to me in a small brown box. It was the only pair of glasses in the famous people's eyeglasses museum saying that they were actually hers. The glasses came with a small card with her signature in it.

Barbara Stanwyck was an American Actress. She was a film and television star, known during her 60-year career as a consummate and versatile professional with a strong, realistic screen presence, and a favorite of directors including Cecil B. DeMille, Fritz Lang and Frank Capra.

After a short but notable career as a stage actress in the late 1920s, she made 85 films in 38 years in Hollywood, before turning to television.

Orphaned at the age of four and partially raised in foster homes, by 1944 Stanwyck had become the highest paid woman in the United States. She was nominated for the Academy Award four times, and won three Emmy Awards and a Golden Globe. She was the recipient of honorary lifetime awards from the Academy of Motion Picture Arts and Sciences in 1981, the American Film institute in 1987, the Film Society of Lincoln Center, the Golden Globes, the Los Angeles Film Critics Association, and the Screen Actors Guild. Stanwyck has a star on the Hollywood Walk of Fame and is ranked as the 11th greatest female star of all time by the American Film Institute.

Stanwyck became a Broadway star soon after when she was cast in her first leading role in *Burlesque* in 1927. She got rave reviews and it was a huge hit. Film actor Pat O'Brien would later say on a talk show, in the 1960s, 'the greatest Broadway show I ever saw was a play in the 1920s called *'Burlesque'*.

She married Frank Fay on August 26, 1928. They adopted a son Dion Anthony Fay and divorced on December 30, 1935. She became involved with Robert Taylor in 1936 and were together until 1950. She never remarried after Robert Taylor, but had a romantic relationship with Robert Wagner in 1953.

Stanwyck died on January 20, 1990 of congestive heart failure and chronic obstructive pulmonary disease at age 82 at Saint John's Health Center. She had indicated that she wished no funeral service. In accordance with her wishes, her remains were created and the ashes scattered from a helicopter over Lone Pine, California, where she had made some of her western films.[111]

RAYMOND BURR

Birth name:	Raymond William Stacey Burr
Born:	May 21, 1917
	New Westminister, British
	Columbia, Canada
Died:	September 12, 1993 (aged 76)
	Healdsburg, California, US
Occupation:	Actor
Years Active:	1940-1993
Spouse(s):	Isabella Ward (m. 1948-1952) divorced
Partner(s):	Robert Benevides (1960-1952) his death

Raymond Burr and Perry Mason was one of the same. He was one of the several gay people that was married as a cover to protect his image as a straight man. In that era, a lot of gays stayed in the closet.

Raymond William Stacey Burr was a Canadian actor, primarily known for his title roles in the television dramas *Perry Mason* and *Ironside*.

His early acting career included roles on Broadway, radio, television and in film, usually as the villain. He won two Emmy Awards in 1959 and 1961 for the role of Perry Mason, which he played for nine seasons between 1957 and 1966. His second hit series, *"Ironside"* earned him six Emmy nominations, and two Golden Globe nominations. He is also widely known for his role as Steve Martin in both *Godzilla, King of the Monsters!* and *Godzilla 1985.*

In addition to acting, Burr owned an orchid business and had begun to grow a vineyard. He was a collector of wines and art, and was very fond of cooking. He was also a dedicated seashell collector whose financial support and gift of cowries and cones from Fiji helped to create the Bailey-Matthews Shell Museum on Sanibel, Florida.

After his death from cancer in 1993, Burr's personal life came into question as details of his known biography appeared to be unverifiable. In 1996, Raymond Burr was ranked #44 on TV Guide's 50 Greatest TV Stars of All Time.

Robert Benevides and Burr owned and operated an orchid business and then a vineyard, in the Dry Creek Valley. They were partners until Burr's death in 1993. Burr left Benevides his entire estate, including "all my jewelry, clothing, books, works of art and other items of a personal nature."

Later accounts of Burr's life explain that he hid his homosexuality to protect his career.[112]

```
DEAR FRIEND,

I AM SO SORRY I COULDN'T GET THE ENCLOSED TO YOU
SOONER AND AS YOU CAN SEE, I'VE HAD ASSISTANCE
ADDRESSING THIS PHOTO.  I APOLOGIZE FOR THIS
NECESSITY.....DUE TO A HAND INJURY - BUT, I HAVE
SIGNED THE PHOTO, PERSONALLY.
```

PEARL BAILEY

Birth name:	Pearl Mae Bailey
Born:	March 29, 1918
	Southampton County, Virginia, U.S.
Died:	August 17, 1990 (aged 72)
	Philadelphia, Pennsylvania, U.S.
Occupation:	Actress, singer
Years Active:	1946-1989
Spouse(s):	John Randolph Pinkett (m.1948-1952)
	Louie Bellson (m 1952-1990)

I thought this was nice of Pearl to write such a sweet letter. We have the letter, but no glasses.

Pearl Mae Bailey was an American actress and singer. After appearing in vaudeville, she made her Broadway debut in *St Louis Woman* in 1946. She won a Tony Award for the title role in the all-black production of *Hello, Dolly!* in 1968. In 1986, she won a Daytime Emmy award for her performance as a fairy godmother in the ABC Afterschool Special, *Cindy Eller: A Modern Fairy Tale.*

Her rendition of *"Takes Two to Tango"* hit the top ten in 1952.

In 1954, she took the role of Frankie in the film version of *Carmen Jones,* and her rendition of "Beat Out That Rhythm on the Drum" is one of the highlights of the film. She also starred in the Broadway musical *House of Flowers*. In 1959, she played the role of Maria in the film version of *Porgy and Bess,* starring Sidney Poitier and Dorothy Dandridge. Also that year, she played the role of Aunt Hagar in the movie *St. Louis Blues*, alongside Mahalia Jackson, Eartha Kitt, and Nat King Cole. Though she was originally considered for the part of Annie Johnson in the 1959 film *Limitation of Life*, the part went to Juanita Moore, for which Moore received an Academy Award nomination.

A passionate fan of the New York Mets, Bailey sang the national anthem at Shea Stadium prior to game 5 of the 1969 World Series, and appeared in the Series highlight film showing her support for the team. She also sang the national anthem prior to game 1 of the 1981 World Series between the New York Yankees and Los Angeles Dodgers at Yankee Stadium.

In her later years Bailey wrote several books: *"The Raw Pearl"* in 1968, *"Talking to Myself"* in 1971, *"Pearl's Kitchen"* in 1973 and *"Hurry Up America and Spit"* in 1976. In 1975 she was appointed special ambassador to the United Nations by President Gerald Ford. She enrolled in Georgetown University and, at age 67, graduated with a Bachelor's Degree in Theology. Her last book, *Between You and Me* in 1989, details her experiences with higher education. On January 19, 1985, she appeared on the nationally televised broadcast of the 50th Presidential Inaugural Gala, the night before the second inauguration of Ronald Reagan. In 1988 Bailey received the Presidential Medal of Freedom from President Reagan.[113]

Melvin J. Bagley

Dear Doc Bagley,

Thanks so much for your nice letter. It must be quite interesting collecting glasses. Unfortunately, I have none to contribute, but I wish you luck with your idea.

Sincerely,

Pearl Bailey

JAMES THURBER

Birth name:	James Grover Thurber
Born:	December 8, 1894
	Columbus, Ohio, US
Died:	November 2, 1961 (Aged 66)
	New York City, New York, US
Occupation:	Humorist
Natioanality:	American
Period:	1929-1961
Genres:	Short Stories, Cartoons and Essays
Notable Works:	*My life and Hard Times, My World and Welcome to It*

> I felt bad for asking for eyeglasses from someone who is no longer alive, but that was a nice gesture of his wife Helen to write to me a nice letter.

James Grover Thurber was an American author, cartoonist and celebrated wit. Thurber was best known for his cartoons and short stories, published mainly in *The New York Magazine* and collected in his numerous books. One of the most popular humorists of his time, Thurber celebrated the comic frustrations and eccentricities of ordinary people.

Thurber was married twice. In 1922, Thurber married Althea Adams. The marriage was troubled and ended in divorce in May 1935. They had a daughter Rosemary together, and lived in Fairfield County, Connecticut. Thurber remarried in June 1935 to Helen Wismer. He was a great lover of dogs, and competed widely in dog shows with several poodles.

He died in 1961, at the age of 66, due to complications from pneumonia, which followed upon a stroke suffered at his home. His last words, aside from the repeated word "God, were God bless… God damn," according to Helen Thurber.

In addition to his other fiction, Thurber wrote over seventy-five fables, most of which were collected in *Fables for Our Time & Famous Poems Illustrated* in 1940 and *Further Fables for Our Time* in 1956. These were short, featured anthropomorphic animals as main characters, and ended with a moral as a tagline. An exception to this format was his most famous fable. *"The Unicorn in the Garden,"* which featured an all-human cast except for the unicorn, which didn't speak. Thurber's fables were satirical, and the morals served as punch lines rather than advice to the reader.[114]

Director

MJB/cmh

Dear Mr. Bagley,
    My husband, James Thurber, died on November 2, 1961. You must have missed the newspapers since their front pages all over the country carried the story of his death.
                Yours truly,
                    Helen W. Thurber

BIRCH BAYH

United States Senator from Indiana

Birth name:	Birch Evans Bayh Jr.
Born:	January 22, 1928
	Terre Haute, Indiana
Nationality:	American
Political party:	Democratic
Spouse(s):	Marvella Hern (1952-1979, her death)
	Katherine "Kitty" Halpin (since 1981)
Children:	Even Bayh (born 1955)
	Christopher Bayh (born 1982)
Residence:	Easton, Maryland
Alma mater:	Purdue University
	Indiana State University
	Indiana University Maurer
	School of Law
Profession:	Politician, Attorney
Service/branch:	United States Army
Years of Service:	1946-1948

Birch Evans Bayh, Jr. is a former United States Senator from Indiana who served from 1963 to 1981. He is the only non-founding father to author two amendments to the United States Constitution and was a candidate for the Democratic nomination for president in 1976. He is the father of former Indiana Governor and former U.S.

Senator Evan Bayh and Christopher Bayh, a lawyer in Washington, D.C.

After President Dwight Eisenhower's health issues in the 1950s, Congress began studying the Constitutions dangerously weak and vague provisions for presidential disability and vice presidential succession. The 1963 assassination of President John F. Kennedy brought a new urgency to the matter. Bayh introduced an amendment on December 12, 1963, which was studied and then re-introduced and passed in 1965 with Emanuel Celler, chairman of the House Judiciary Committee. The resulting Twenty-fifth Amendment to the United States Constitution, ratified in 1967, created a process for an orderly transition of power in the case of death, disability, or resignation of the President, and a method of selecting a Vice President when a vacancy occurs in that office. It has since been invoked six times, most notably in the 1973 vice presidential and 1974 presidential succession of Gerald Ford.[115]

United States Senate

COMMITTEE ON APPROPRIATIONS

WASHINGTON, D.C. 20510

Dr. M. J. Bagley
Director
Famous People's Eye Glasses Museum
61 East Lake Mead Drive
Henderson, Nevada 89015

Dear Dr. Bagley:

Thank you for your request for a pair of my
eye glasses.

At the present time I have two pairs of glasses --
one for my office and one for my home. I have no extra
pairs or old pairs, but at the time I decide to replace
either one of the pairs I now have, it will be my pleasure
to forward a pair to your museum.

Thank you again for your interest in me and including
my glasses in your museum.

Sincerely,

Birch Bayh

Birch Bayh
United States Senator

WHOOPI GOLDBERG

Birth name:	Caryn Elaine Johnson
Born:	November 13, 1955
	New York City, New York, US
Occupation:	Actress, comedienne, radio disc jockey, producer, author, singer-songwriter, talk show host, Broadway star
Years Active:	1981 – present
Spouse(s):	Alvin "Louise" Martin (m.1973-79) divorced
	David Claessen (m. 1968-88) divorced
	Lyle Trachtenberg (m. 1994-95) divorced
Partner(s):	Frank Langella (1996-2001)

Whoopi! That is what we were all saying in my office the day we received her eyeglasses.

Caryn Elaine Johnson, best known as Whoopi Goldberg is an American comedienne, actress, singer-songwriter, political activist, author and talk show host.

Goldberg made her film debut in *The Color Purple* in 1985, playing Celie, a mistreated black woman in the Deep South. She received a nomination for the Academy Award for Best Actress and won her first Golden Globe Award for her role in the film. In 1990, she played Oda Mae Brown, a wacky psychic helping a slain man Patrick Swayze save his lover Demi Moore in the blockbuster *Ghost*. This performance won her a second Golden Globe and an Academy Award for Best Supporting Actress, this made Goldberg only the second black woman in the history of the Academy Awards to win an acting Oscar. The first one was Hattie McDaniel who won for *Gone With the Wind* in 1939. Notable later films include *Sister Act* and *Sister Act 2*, "*The Player Made in America*," *How Stella Got Her Groove Back*," "*Girl, Interrupted*," and *Rat Race*. She is also acclaimed for her roles as the bartender Guinan in *Star Trek: The Next Generation*, as Terry Doolittle in *Jumpin' Jack Flash*, and as Carmen Tibideaux in *Glee*, as well as the voice of Shenzi the hyena in *The Lion King*.

Goldberg has been nominated for 13 Emmy Awards for her work in television. She was co-producer of the popular game show Hollywood Squares from 1998 to 2004. She has been the moderator of the daytime talk show *The View* since 2007. Goldberg has a Grammy, two Daytime Emmys, two Golden Globes, a Tony for production, not acting, and an Oscar. In addition, Goldberg has a British Academy Film Award, four People's Choice Awards, and has been honored with a star on the Hollywood Walk of Fame. She is one of the few entertainers who have won an Emmy, Grammy, Oscar, and Tony Award.

Goldberg has been married three times, in 1973 to Alvin Martin and they divorced in 1979. They had one daughter in 1986. Next she was married to cinematographer David Claessen, they divorced in 1988, and in 1994 to the actor Lyle Trachtenburg and they divorced in 1995. She has also been romantically linked with actor Frank Langella and Ted Danson.[116]

WHOOP, INC.
4000 Warner Boulevard, WEA #405
Burbank, California 91505
(818) 840-6212

November 23, 1987

Dr. M. J. Bagley
FAMOUS PEOPLE'S EYE GLASSES MUSEUM
61 East Lake Mead Drive
Box 775
Henderson, NV 89015

Dear Dr. Bagley:

Enclosed please find a pair of sunglasses from Whoopi
Goldberg. They are her own, you can tell by the teeth
marks on the ear piece of the frame.

Best wishes for continued success. If there is any
information about the museum or photos, Whoopi would
like to have it for her scrapbook.

Best regards,

Ron Holder

Enclosure

COLONEL SANDERS

Birth name:	Harland David Sanders
Born:	September 9, 1890
	Henryville, Indiana, US
Died:	December 16, 1980 (aged 90)
	Louisville, Kentucky, US
Cause of Death:	Complication from pneumonia and leukemia
Nationality:	American
Occupation:	Entrepreneur
Founder:	Kentucky Fried Chicken
Religion:	Disciples of Christ
Spouses:	Josephine King and Caludia Price
Children:	Harland David Sanders, Jr., Margaret Sanders, Mildred Sanders Ruggles

Somehow or another we misplaced Colonel Harland Sanders letter with his glasses. His glasses sit in my museum.

Colonel Harland David Sanders was an American businessman, restaurateur, and goodwill ambassador for KFC. Sanders held a number of jobs in his early life including fireman, insurance salesman and running filing stations. He began selling fried chicken from his roadside restaurant in Corbin, Kentucky during the Great Depression. Sanders was one of the first people to see the potential of the restaurant franchising concept, with the first "Kentucky Fried Chicken" franchise opening in Utah in 1952. The franchise popularized chicken in the fast food industry, thereby diversifying the market and challenging the dominance of the hamburger. Marketing himself as "Colonel Sanders," he became a legendary figure of American cultural history, and his image is still prominently used in KFC branding. The company's rapid expansion saw it grow too large for Sanders to manage, and in 1964 he sold the company to a group of investors led by John Y. Brown, Jr. and Jack Massey.[117]

ELIZABETH HOLTZMAN

Born:	August 11, 1941
	Brooklyn, New York
Political party:	Democratic
Alma Mater:	Radcliffe College, Harvard Law School
Profession:	Lawyer
Committees:	House Judiciary Committee and House Budget Committee
Religion:	Judaism

Elizabeth Holtzman born is an American politician and former member of the United States House of Representatives. She is the youngest woman to have been elected to the United States Congress, and the first woman to hold office as the New York City Comptroller, and the District Attorney of Kings County, New York. A Democrat, she represented New York's 16th congressional district for four teams.

In 1974, she drew national media attention as a member of the House Judiciary Committee, which recommended three articles of impeachment against Richard Nixon during the Watergate scandal. After Nixon resigned as president and was given a presidential pardon by his successor, Gerard Ford the judiciary committee held hearings on the pardon. Hortzman asked Ford whether his action had been a quid pro quo.

She is the daughter of attorney Sidney Holtzman and Filia Holtzman who was a college professor. She graduated from Brooklyn's Abraham Lincoln High School in 1958 and Radcliffe College, magna cum Laude in 1962, and Harvard Law School in 1965. She was admitted to the bar in New York State in 1966.

She now has her private practice after her last term in 1994 and is an author on politics in New York City.[118]

ELIZABETH HOLTZMAN
16TH DISTRICT, BROOKLYN, NEW YORK

BROOKLYN OFFICE:
1428 FLATBUSH AVENUE
BROOKLYN, NEW YORK 11210
PHONE (212) 859-9111

WASHINGTON OFFICE:
2238 RAYBURN BUILDING
WASHINGTON, D.C. 20515
PHONE (202) 225-6616

Congress of the United States
House of Representatives
Washington, D.C. 20515

COMMITTEES:
JUDICIARY
CHAIRWOMAN, SUBCOMMITTEE ON
IMMIGRATION, REFUGEES, AND
INTERNATIONAL LAW

BUDGET
CHAIRWOMAN, TASK FORCE ON STATE
AND LOCAL GOVERNMENT

February 3, 1981

Dear Dr. Bagley,

Enclosed is a pair of glasses that I did, indeed, wear.

I am pleased that you wish to include them in your FAMOUS PEOPLE'S EYEGLASSES MUSEUM.

Thank you so much for your interest.

Sincerely,
Elizabeth Holtzman

THIS STATIONERY PRINTED ON PAPER MADE WITH RECYCLED FIBERS

CHARLES HAMILTON

Born:	1914
	Ludington, Michigan,
Died:	December 11, 1996
	New York City, New York

Charles Hamilton studied English literature and served in the military before creating a dealership out of his passion—collecting famous autographs. He also became a sought-after handwriting expert, able to verify the works of Shakespeare and that the Hitler diaries were a fake. He is the author of books like *American Autographs*.

In 1942, Charles Hamilton enlisted in the U.S. Army Air Corps. He served in World War II, winning a bronze star and six battle stars before completing his tour of duty in 1945.

Returning home to New York City, Hamilton pursued a personal hobby that would greatly influence his later career: He began collecting autographs, selling pieces to other collectors from time to time. As his hobby progressed, however, Hamilton realized that becoming a full-time dealer could prove to be lucrative career and in the early 1950s, started a business selling collectibles-various items, but mostly rare autographs and letters penned by both famous and infamous individuals, from historical figures to serial killers to celebrities. Soon, he was selling his wares at local auctions.

A side effect of his longtime hobby turned trade, Hamilton developed an impressive knack for identifying handwriting and autographs and spotting forgeries. Soon, he became credited as an expert authority in graphology, the study and analysis of handwriting which includes analyses of written works for the purpose of gaining insight into a writer's psyche.

Thusly, Hamilton was engaged in several notable controversial cases throughout his career, including the investigation of the infamous Zodiac Killer, who committed a string of murder in the San Francisco Bay area in the late 1960s and early70s. Working with the New York Police Department, Hamilton served as a consultant on the Zodiac case.

In 1963, Hamilton established Charles Hamilton Galleries in New York City, the first American gallery devoted exclusively to autographs.[119]

Celebrity Sighting

CHARLES HAMILTON

Galleries Inc.

25 EAST 77th ST., NEW YORK 10021
(AT MADISON AVENUE)
Tel: (212) 628-1666-7-8

Fine Autographs of Interest and Importance

November 19
1 9 8 1

Dr. M.J. Bagley, Director
Famous People's Eye Glasses Museum
61 East Lake Mead Drive
Henderson, Nev. 89015

Dear Dr. Bagley:

Early this year you wrote and asked for a pair of my old
eye glasses. The only ones I could find were those currently in use, but just a few minutes ago I ran across
the enclosed flamboyant spectacles. I put them on and my
wife looked at me and dissolved into hysterical laughter.

I wore these glasses for several years, hoping that someone would mistake me for Marlon Brando. I even tried to
look tough but nobody fell for it.

So here they are. If you decide to display them, I sug-
gest the darkest corner you have in your museum.

Cordially,

Charles Hamilton

ENDNOTES

1. Wikipedia, "Ronald Reagan." Last modified 09 09, 2013. Accessed September 9, 2013, http://en.wikipedia.org/wiki/Reagan.

2. Wikipedia, "Faith Baldwin." Last modified 09 09, 2013. Accessed September 9, 2013, http://en.wikipedia.org/wiki/Faith Baldwin

3. Wikipedia, "Irving Berlin." Last modified 09 09, 2013. Accessed September 9, 2013, http://en.wikipedia.org/wiki/Irving Berlin.

4. Wikipedia, "Eleanor Roosevelt." Last modified 09 09, 2013. Accessed September 9, 2013, http://en.wikipedia.org/wiki/Eleanor Roosevelt.

5. Wikipedia, "Pearl S. Buck." Last modified 09 09, 2013. Accessed September 9, 2013, http://en.wikipedia.org/wiki/PearlS.Buck.

6. Wikipedia, "Henry Ford II." Last modified 09 09, 2013. Accessed September 9, 2013,http://en.wikipedia.org/wiki/HenryFordII.

7. Wikipedia, "Nat King Cole." Last modified 09 09, 2013. Accessed September 9, 2013, http://en.wikipedia.org/wiki/Nat_King_Cole.

8. Wikipedia, "Bing Crosby." Last modified 09 09, 2013. Accessed September 9, 2013, http://en.wikipedia.org/wiki/BingCrosby.

9. Wikipedia, "Greer Garson." Last modified 09 09, 2013. Accessed September 9, 2013, http://en.wikipedia.org/wiki/GreerGarson.

10. Wikipedia, "Hedda Hopper." Last modified 09 09, 2013. Accessed September 9, 2013, http://en.wikipedia.org/wiki/HeddaHopper.

11. Wikipedia, "Jennifer Jones." Last modified 09 09, 2013. Accessed September 9, 2013, http://en.wikipedia.org/wiki/Jennifer Jones

12. Wikipedia, "David O. Selznick." Last modified 09 09, 2013. Accessed September 9, 2013, http://en.wikipedia.org/wiki/David O. Selznick.

13. Wikipedia, "Helen Hayes." Last modified 09 09, 2013. Accessed September 9, 2013, http://en.wikipedia.org/wiki/Helen Hayes..

14. Wikipedia, "J Edgar Hoover." Last modified 09 09, 2013. Accessed September 9, 2013, http://en.wikipedia.org/wiki/J Edgar Hoover.

15. Wikipedia, "Drew Pearson." Last modified 09 09, 2013. Accessed September 9, 2013, http://en.wikipedia.org/wiki/Drew Pearson.

16. Wikipedia, "Duncan Hines." Last modified 09 09, 2013. Accessed September 9, 2013, http://en.wikipedia.org/wiki/Duncan Hines.

17. Wikipedia, "Gene Kelly." Last modified 09 09, 2013. Accessed September 9, 2013, http://en.wikipedia.org/wiki/Gene Kelly.

18. Wikipedia, "Ozzie Nelson." Last modified 09 09, 2013. Accessed September 9, 2013, http://en.wikipedia.org/wiki/Ozzie Nelson.

19. Wikipedia, "Edward R. Murrow." Last modified 09 09, 2013. Accessed September 9, 2013, http://en.wikipedia. org/wiki/Edward R. Murrow.

20. Wikipedia, "Cary Grant." Last modified 09 09, 2013. Accessed September 9, 2013, http://en.wikipedia.org/ wiki/Cary Grant.

21. Wikipedia, "Alfred Hitchcock." Last modified 09 09, 2013. Accessed September 9, 2013, http://en.wikipedia. org/wiki/Alfred Hitchcock.

22. Wikipedia, "Richard Rodgers." Last modified 09 09, 2013. Accessed September 9, 2013, http://en.wikipedia. org/wiki/Richard Rodgers.

23. Wikipedia, "Cole Porter." Last modified 09 09, 2013. Accessed September 9, 2013, http://en.wikipedia.org/ wiki/Cole Porter.

24. Wikipedia, "Emily Post." Last modified 09 09, 2013. Accessed September 9, 2013,http://en.wikipedia.org/ wiki/Emily Post.

25. Wikipedia, "Helena Rubinstein." Last modified 09 09, 2013. Accessed September 9, 2013, http://en.wikipedia. org/wiki/Helena_Rubinstein

26 . Wikipedia, "Lawrence Welk." Last modified 09 09, 2013. Accessed September 9, 2013, http://en.wikipedia. org/wiki/Lawrence_Welk

27. Wikipedia, "Ann Sothern." Last modified 09 09, 2013. Accessed September 9, 2013, http://en.wikipedia.org/ wiki/Ann_Sothern

28. Wikipedia, "Peggy Lee." Last modified 09 09, 2013. Accessed September 9, 2013, http://en.wikipedia.org/ wiki/Peggy_Lee

29. Wikipedia, "Dean Rusk" Last modified 09 09, 2013. Accessed September 9, 2013, http://en.wikipedia.org/wiki/Dean_Rusk

30. Wikipedia, "Garry Moore." Last modified 09 09, 2013. Accessed September 9, 2013, http://en.wikipedia.org/wiki/Garry_Moore

31. Wikipedia, "Ulysses S. Grant." Last modified 09 09, 2013. Accessed September 9, 2013, http://en.wikipedia.org/wiki/Ulysses S. Grant

32. Wikipedia, "Jack Lemmon." Last modified 09 09, 2013. Accessed September 9, 2013, http://en.wikipedia.org/wiki/Jack_Lemmon

33. Wikipedia, "Erle Stanley Gardner" Last modified 09 09, 2013. Accessed September 9, 2013, http://en.wikipedia.org/wiki/Erle_Stanley_Gardner

34. Wikipedia, "Mel Allen." Last modified 09 09, 2013. Accessed September 9, 2013, http://en.wikipedia.org/wiki/Mel_Allen

35. Wikipedia, "Pat Boone." Last modified 09 09, 2013. Accessed September 9, 2013, http://en.wikipedia.org/wiki/Pat_Boone

36. Wikipedia, "Carol Burnett." Last modified 09 09, 2013. Accessed September 9, 2013, http://en.wikipedia.org/wiki/Carol_Burnett

37. Wikipedia, "Noel Coward." Last modified 09 09, 2013. Accessed September 9, 2013, http://en.wikipedia.org/wiki/Noel_Coward

38. Wikipedia, "Jimmy Doolittle." Last modified 09 09, 2013. Accessed September 9, 2013, http://en.wikipedia.org/wiki/Jimmy_Doolittle

39. Wikipedia, "Betty Furness." Last modified 09 09, 2013. Accessed September 9, 2013, http://en.wikipedia.org/wiki/Betty_Furness

40. Wikipedia, "Agatha Christie." Last modified 09 09, 2013. Accessed September 9, 2013, http://en.wikipedia.org/wiki/Agatha_Christie

41. Wikipedia, "William O. Douglas." Last modified 09 09, 2013. Accessed September 9, 2013, http://en.wikipedia.org/wiki/William_O_Douglas

42. Wikipedia, "Walter Cronkite." Last modified 09 09, 2013. Accessed September 9, 2013, http://en.wikipedia.org/wiki/Walter_Cronkite

43. Wikipedia, "Herb Shriner." Last modified 09 09, 2013. Accessed September 9, 2013, http://en.wikipedia.org/wiki/Herb_Shriner

44. Wikipedia, "Conrad Hilton." Last modified 09 09, 2013. Accessed September 9, 2013, http://en.wikipedia.org/wiki/Conrad_Hilton

45. Wikipedia, "Robert F. Kennedy." Last modified 09 09, 2013. Accessed September 9, 2013, http://en.wikipedia.org/wiki/Robert_F_Kennedy

46. Wikipedia, "Kim Hunter." Last modified 09 09, 2013. Accessed September 9, 2013, http://en.wikipedia.org/wiki/Kim_Hunter

47. Wikipedia, "Princess Margaret, Countess of Snowdon." Last modified 09 09, 2013. Accessed September 9, 2013, http://en.wikipedia.org/wiki/Princess_Margaret,_Countess_of_Snowdon

48. Wikipedia, "Jayne Mansfield." Last modified 09 09, 2013. Accessed September 9, 2013, http://en.wikipedia.org/wiki/Jayne_Mansfield

49. Wikipedia, "Barry Goldwater." Last modified 09 09, 2013. Accessed September 9, 2013, http://en.wikipedia. org/wiki/Barry_Goldwater

50. Wikipedia, "Leon Jaworski." Last modified 09 09, 2013. Accessed September 9, 2013, http://en.wikipedia.org/ wiki/Leon_Jaworski

51. Wikipedia, "Edward G. Robinson." Last modified 09 09, 2013. Accessed September 9, 2013, http://en.wikipedia. org/wiki/Edward_G_Robinson

52. Wikipedia, "Red Skelton." Last modified 09 09, 2013. Accessed September 9, 2013, http://en.wikipedia.org/ wiki/Red_Skelton

53. Wikipedia, "Robert Frost." Last modified 09 09, 2013. Accessed September 9, 2013, http://en.wikipedia.org/ wiki/Robert _Frost

54. Wikipedia, "Steve Allen." Last modified 09 09, 2013. Accessed September 9, 2013, http://en.wikipedia.org/ wiki/Steve_Allen

55. Wikipedia, "Henry Cabot Lodge Jr." Last modified 09 09, 2013. Accessed September 9, 2013, http:// en.wikipedia.org/wiki/Henry_Cabot_Lodge_Jr.

56. Wikipedia, "Kyle Rote." Last modified 09 09, 2013. Accessed September 9, 2013, http://en.wikipedia.org/ wiki/Kyle_Rote

57. Wikipedia, "Vanessa Redgrave." Last modified 09 09, 2013. Accessed September 9, 2013, http://en.wikipedia. org/wiki/Vanessa_Redgrave

58. Wikipedia, "Julie Christie." Last modified 09 09, 2013. Accessed September 9, 2013, http://en.wikipedia.org/ wiki/Julie_Christie

59. Wikipedia, "Ed Begley." Last modified 09 09, 2013. Accessed September 9, 2013, http://en.wikipedia.org/wiki/Ed_Begley

60. Wikipedia, "Kaye Ballard." Last modified 09 09, 2013. Accessed September 9, 2013, http://en.wikipedia.org/wiki/Kaye_Ballard

61. Wikipedia, "Anne Baxter." Last modified 09 09, 2013. Accessed September 9, 2013, http://en.wikipedia.org/wiki/Anne_Baxter

62. Wikipedia, "Phyllis Diller." Last modified 09 09, 2013. Accessed September 9, 2013, http://en.wikipedia.org/wiki/Phyllis_Diller

63. Wikipedia, "Robert Goulet." Last modified 09 09, 2013. Accessed September 9, 2013, http://en.wikipedia.org/wiki/Robert_Goulet

64. Wikipedia, "Paul Anka." Last modified 09 09, 2013. Accessed September 9, 2013, http://en.wikipedia.org/wiki/Paul_Anka

65. Wikipedia, "Artie Shaw." Last modified 09 09, 2013. Accessed September 9, 2013, http://en.wikipedia.org/wiki/Artie_Shaw

66. Wikipedia, "Peter Sellers." Last modified 09 09, 2013. Accessed September 9, 2013, http://en.wikipedia.org/wiki/Peter_Sellers

67. Wikipedia, "Lillian Gish." Last modified 09 09, 2013. Accessed September 9, 2013, http://en.wikipedia.org/wiki/Lillian_Gish

68. Wikipedia, "Jimmy Durante." Last modified 09 09, 2013. Accessed September 9, 2013, http://en.wikipedia.org/wiki/Jimmy_Durante

69. Wikipedia, "Douglas Fairbanks, Jr." Last modified 09 09, 2013. Accessed September 9, 2013, http://en.wikipedia.org/wiki/Douglas_Fairbanks_Jr

70. Wikipedia, "Ted Mack." Last modified 09 09, 2013. Accessed September 9, 2013, http://en.wikipedia.org/wiki/Ted_Mack

71. Wikipedia, "Loretta Lynn." Last modified 09 09, 2013. Accessed September 9, 2013, http://en.wikipedia.org/wiki/Loretta_Lynn

72. Wikipedia, "Carl Albert." Last modified 09 09, 2013. Accessed September 9, 2013, http://en.wikipedia.org/wiki/Carl_Albert

73. Wikipedia, "Hugh Downs." Last modified 09 09, 2013. Accessed September 9, 2013, http://en.wikipedia.org/wiki/Hugh_Downs

74. Wikipedia, "Roger Staubach." Last modified 09 09, 2013. Accessed September 9, 2013, http://en.wikipedia.org/wiki/Roger_Staubach

75. Wikipedia, "William Rehnquist." Last modified 09 09, 2013. Accessed September 9, 2013, http://en.wikipedia.org/wiki/William_Rehnquist

76. Wikipedia, "Spiro Agnew." Last modified 09 09, 2013. Accessed September 9, 2013, http://en.wikipedia.org/wiki/Spiro_Agnew

77. Wikipedia, "Melvyn Douglas." Last modified 09 09, 2013. Accessed September 9, 2013, http://en.wikipedia.org/wiki/Melvyn_Douglas

78. Wikipedia, "Don McLean." Last modified 09 09, 2013. Accessed September 9, 2013, http://en.wikipedia.org/wiki/Don_McLean

79. Wikipedia, "Ryan O'Neal." Last modified 09 09, 2013. Accessed September 9, 2013, http://en.wikipedia.org/wiki/Ryan_O%27Neal

80. Wikipedia, "Henry Kissinger." Last modified 09 09, 2013. Accessed September 9, 2013, http://en.wikipedia.org/wiki/Henry_Kissinger

81. Wikipedia, "Anwar Sadat." Last modified 09 09, 2013. Accessed September 9, 2013, http://en.wikipedia.org/wiki/Anwar_Sadat

82. Wikipedia, "Philip K. Wrigley." Last modified 09 05, 2013. Accessed September 5, 2013. http://en.wikipedia.org/wiki/Philip_Knight_Wrigley.

83. Wikipedia, "Margaret Thatcher." Last modified 09 05, 2013. Accessed September 5, 2013. http://en.wikipedia.org/wiki/Margaret_Thatcher.

84. Wikipedia, "Maurice Strong." Last modified 09 05, 2013. Accessed September 5, 2013. http://en.wikipedia.org/wiki/Maurice_Strong.

85. Wikipedia, "Goddard Lieberson." Last modified 09 05, 2013. Accessed September 5, 2013. http://en.wikipedia.org/wiki/Goddard_Lieberson.

86. Wikipedia, "Lili Kraus." Last modified 09 05, 2013. Accessed September 5, 2013. http://en.wikipedia.org/wiki/Lili_Kraus.

87. Wikipedia, "Peter Bogdanovich." Last modified 09 05, 2013. Accessed September 5, 2013. http://en.wikipedia.org/wiki/Peter_Bogdanovich.

88. Wikipedia, "Gussie Busch." Last modified 09 05, 2013. Accessed September 5, 2013. http://en.wikipedia.org/wiki/Gussie_Busch.

89. Wikipedia, "Buckminster Fuller." Last modified 09 05, 2013. Accessed September 5, 2013. http://en.wikipedia.org/wiki/Buckminster_Fuller.

90. Wikipedia, "William Ball." Last modified 09 05, 2013. Accessed September 5, 2013. http://en.wikipedia.org/wiki/William_Ball.

91. Wikipedia, "Stanley Dancer." Last modified 09 05, 2013. Accessed September 5, 2013. http://en.wikipedia.org/wiki/Stanley_Dancer.

92. Wikipedia, "Jean Stapleton." Last modified 09 05, 2013. Accessed September 5, 2013. http://en.wikipedia.org/wiki/Jean_Stapleton.

93. Wikipedia, "Pierre Andrew Rinfret." Last modified 09 05, 2013. Accessed September 5, 2013. http://en.wikipedia.org/wiki/Pierre_Andrew_Rinfret.

94. Wikipedia, "Thomas Hinman Moorer." Last modified 09 05, 2013. Accessed September 5, 2013. http://en.wikipedia.org/wiki/Thomas_Hinman_Moorer.

95. Wikipedia, "Giles Gordan." Last modified 09 05, 2013. Accessed September 5, 2013. http://en.wikipedia.org/wiki/Giles_Gordan.

96. Wikipedia, "Michael Tippett." Last modified 09 05, 2013. Accessed September 5, 2013. http://en.wikipedia.org/wiki/Michael_Tippett.

97. Wikipedia, "William Ruckelshaus." Last modified 09 05, 2013. Accessed September 5, 2013. http://en.wikipedia.org/wiki/William_Ruckelshaus.

98. Wikipedia, "Gus Hall." Last modified 09 05, 2013. Accessed September 5, 2013. http://en.wikipedia.org/wiki/Gus_Hall.

99. Wikipedia, "Fred Rogers." Last modified 09 05, 2013. Accessed September 5, 2013. http://en.wikipedia.org/wiki/Fred_Rogers.

100. Wikipedia, "Richard M. Scammon." Last modified 09 05, 2013. Accessed September 5, 2013. http://en.wikipedia.org/wiki/Richard_M._Scammon.

101. Wikipedia, "Erica Jong." Last modified 09 05, 2013. Accessed September 5, 2013. http://en.wikipedia.org/wiki/Erica _Jong.

102. Wikipedia, "Milos Forman." Last modified 09 05, 2013. Accessed September 5, 2013. http://en.wikipedia.org/wiki/Milos_Forman.

103. Wikipedia, "Paul Simon." Last modified 09 05, 2013. Accessed September 5, 2013. http://en.wikipedia.org/wiki/Paul_Simon.

104. Wikipedia, "Daniel Bell." Last modified 09 05, 2013. Accessed September 5, 2013. http://en.wikipedia.org/wiki/Daniel _Bell.

105. Wikipedia, "Betty White." Last modified 09 05, 2013. Accessed September 5, 2013. http://en.wikipedia.org/wiki/Betty_white.

106. Wikipedia, "David L. Wolper." Last modified 09 05, 2013. Accessed September 5, 2013. http://en.wikipedia.org/wiki/David_L._Wolper.

107. Wikipedia, "Norm Crosby." Last modified 09 05, 2013. Accessed September 5, 2013. http://en.wikipedia.org/wiki/Norm_Crosby.

108. Wikipedia, "Liz Claiborne." Last modified 09 05, 2013. Accessed September 5, 2013. http://en.wikipedia.org/wiki/Liz_Claiborne.

109. Wikipedia, "Brooks Robinson." Last modified 09 05, 2013. Accessed September 5, 2013. http://en.wikipedia. org/wiki/Brooks_Robinson.

110. Wikipedia, "Rudy Vallee." Last modified 09 05, 2013. Accessed September 5, 2013. http://en.wikipedia.org/ wiki/Rudy_Vallee.

111. Wikipedia, "Barbara Stanwyck." Last modified 09 05, 2013. Accessed September 5, 2013. http://en.wikipedia. org/wiki/Barbara_Stanwyck.

112. Wikipedia, "Raymond Burr." Last modified 09 05, 2013. Accessed September 5, 2013. http://en.wikipedia.org/ wiki/Raymond_Burr.

113. Wikipedia, "Pearl Bailey." Last modified 09 05, 2013. Accessed September 5, 2013. http://en.wikipedia.org/ wiki/Pearl_Bailey.

114. Wikipedia, "James Thurber." Last modified 09 05, 2013. Accessed September 5, 2013. http://en.wikipedia.org/ wiki/James_Thurber.

115. Wikipedia, "Birch Bayh." Last modified 09 05, 2013. Accessed September 5, 2013. http://en.wikipedia.org/ wiki/Birch_Bayh.

116. Wikipedia, "Whoopi Goldberg." Last modified 09 05, 2013. Accessed September 5, 2013. http://en.wikipedia. org/wiki/Whoopi_Goldberg.

117. Wikipedia, "KFC." Last modified 09 05, 2013. Accessed September 5, 2013. http://en.wikipedia.org/wiki/KFC.

118. Wikipedia, "Elizabeth Holtzman." Last modified 09 05, 2013. Accessed September 5, 2013. http://en.wikipedia. org/wiki/Elizabeth_Holtzman.

119. Wikipedia, "Charles Hamilton." Last modified 09 05, 2013. Accessed September 5, 2013. http://en.wikipedia.org/wiki/Charles_Hamilton.